Everybody Ought to Know

Verses selected and introduced by

OGDEN NASH

Everybody

Illustrations by Rose Shirvanian

J. B. LIPPINCOTT COMPANY
Philadelphia and New York

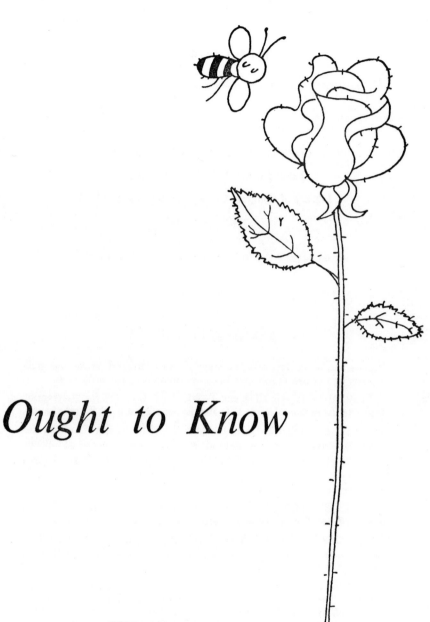

Ought to Know

E761154

ACKNOWLEDGMENTS

Permission to reprint material copyright or controlled by various publishers, agents and individuals has been granted by the following:

THE BODLEY HEAD LTD. and T. WERNER LAURIE for "Cervantes" from *Clerihews Complete* by E. C. Bentley, published by T. Werner Laurie.

CHATTO & WINDUS LTD. for permission to reprint "Anthem for Doomed Youth" from *Poems* by Wilfred Owen in the Dominion of Canada.

CROWN PUBLISHERS for "The Humorist" from *Pot-Shots from Pegasus* by Keith Preston, copyright 1929 by Covici, Friede, Inc., 1957 by Crown Publishers; used by permission of Crown.

J. M. DENT & SONS LTD. for permission to reprint "Fern Hill" from *The Collected Poems of Dylan Thomas* in the Dominion of Canada.

DODD, MEAD & COMPANY for "The Rolling English Road" and "Elegy in a Country Churchyard" from *The Collected Poems of G. K. Chesterton*, copyright 1932 by Dodd, Mead & Company, Inc.

DOUBLEDAY & COMPANY, INC. for "the hen and the oriole," "archy confesses," and "fate is unfair" from *The Lives and Times of Archy and Mehitabel*, by Don Marquis, copyright 1927, 1930, 1933, 1935 by Doubleday and Company, Inc.; "The Looking-Glass" from *Rewards and Fairies*,

4

ACKNOWLEDGMENTS

by Rudyard Kipling, copyright 1910 by Rudyard Kipling; "The Camel's Hump" from *The Just-So Stories,* by Rudyard Kipling, copyright 1912 by Rudyard Kipling; "Mice" from *Fifty-One Nursery Rhymes* by Rose Fyleman, copyright 1932 by Doubleday and Company, Inc.; all used with the permission of Doubleday and Company, Inc.

GERALD DUCKWORTH & COMPANY LTD. for "The Death of Prince Leopold" and "The Tay Bridge Disaster" from *Poetic Gems* by William McGonagall.

DUELL, SLOAN AND PEARCE, INC. for "anyone lived in a pretty how town" from *Fifty Poems,* by e. e. cummings, copyright 1940 by E. E. Cummings.

E. P. DUTTON AND COMPANY, INC. for "The Shakespearean Bear" from *Gaily the Troubadour* by Arthur Guiterman, copyright 1936 by E. P. Dutton & Co., Inc.; "Presents" from *Around and About* by Marchette Chute, copyright 1932 by Marchette Chute, published 1957 by E. P. Dutton & Co., Inc., and reprinted with their permission.

NORMA MILLAY ELLIS for "Recuerdo" from *A Few Figs from Thistles* by Edna St. Vincent Millay, copyright 1922, 1950 by Edna St. Vincent Millay, published by Harper & Brothers.

FABER AND FABER LTD. for permission to reprint "The Rum Tum Tugger" from *Old Possum's Book of Practical Cats* by T. S. Eliot, and "Cape Ann" from *Collected Poems* by T. S. Eliot, in the Dominion of Canada.

HAZEL FETZER for "The Dick Johnson Reel" from *The Bulls of Spring,* by Jake Falstaff, published by G. P. Putnam's Sons.

HARCOURT, BRACE AND WORLD, INC. for "The Rum Tum Tugger" from *Old Possum's Book of Practical Cats* by T. S. Eliot, copyright 1939 by T. S. Eliot; "Cape Ann" from *Collected Poems* by T. S. Eliot, copyright 1936 by Harcourt, Brace and Company, Inc.; "Potomac Town in February" from *Smoke and Steel* by Carl Sandburg, copyright 1920 by Harcourt, Brace and Company, Inc., renewed 1948 by Carl Sandburg; all used by permission of Harcourt, Brace and Company, Inc.

HARPER & BROTHERS for "Chorus" from *Atalanta in Calydon* by Algernon Charles Swinburne.

HOLT, RINEHART & WINSTON, INC. for two verses from *Complete Poems of A. E. Housman,* copyright 1940, © 1959 by Henry Holt and Company, Inc.; "Brown's Descent" and "The Road Not Taken" from *You Come Too* by Robert Frost, copyright 1916, 1921, © 1959 by Henry Holt and Company, Inc., 1942, 1944 by Robert Frost; "One bright morning . . . ," "Way down South . . . ," "Oh, the funniest thing . . . ," and "I

ACKNOWLEDGMENTS

eat my peas with honey . . ." from *A Rocket in My Pocket* by Carl Withers; all used by permission of the publishers.

HOUGHTON MIFFLIN COMPANY for "The Bird's Nest" from *All About Me* by John Drinkwater; "The Man from Porlock" from *Dr. Johnson's Waterfall* by Helen Bevington; both reprinted by permission of Houghton Mifflin Company.

ALFRED A. KNOPF, INC. for "Jim, Who ran away from his Nurse and was Eaten by a Lion," "The Python" and "The Llama" from *Cautionary Verses* by Hilaire Belloc, published 1941 by Alfred A. Knopf, Inc.; "Here Lies a Lady" from *Selected Poems* by John Crowe Ransom, copyright 1924, 1945 by Alfred A. Knopf, Inc.; all used by permission of Alfred A. Knopf, Inc.

J. B. LIPPINCOTT COMPANY for "What You Will Learn about the Brobinyak" and "I Took a Bow and Arrow" from *The Reason for the Pelican* by John Ciardi, copyright © 1959 by John Ciardi, published by J. B. Lippincott Company; "He Comforts Himself," "A Human Instinct," "Secret Thoughts" and "The Man with the Rake" from *Translations from the Chinese*, by Christopher Morley, copyright 1922, 1949 by Christopher Morley, published by J. B. Lippincott Company.

LIVERIGHT PUBLISHING CORPORATION for three verses from "Poems in Praise of Practically Nothing" from *A Treasury of Humorous Verse* by Samuel Hoffenstein, copyright © 1956 by David Hoffenstein, by permission of Liveright Publishers, N.Y.C.

LITTLE, BROWN AND COMPANY for "Old Men" and "The Hunter" from *Verses From 1929 On* by Ogden Nash, both reprinted by permission of the publishers.

THE MACMILLAN COMPANY for "Weathers" and "The Darkling Thrush" from *Collected Poems* by Thomas Hardy, copyright 1925 by The Macmillan Company; "Mr. Flood's Party" from *Collected Poems* by Edwin Arlington Robinson, copyright 1921 by Edwin Arlington Robinson, 1949 by The Macmillan Company; "Eve" from *Poems* by Ralph Hodgson, copyright 1917, 1945 by The Macmillan Company; "An Old Song Resung" from *Collected Poems* by John Masefield, copyright 1912, 1940 by The Macmillan Company; "A Ballad of John Silver" from *Salt Water Ballads* by John Masefield, copyright 1916 by John Masefield, 1944 by The Macmillan Company; "The Moon's the North Wind's Cooky" from *Johnny Appleseed and Other Poems* by Vachel Lindsay, copyright 1914, 1942 by The Macmillan Company; "Seumas Beg" from *Collected Poems* by James Stephens, copyright 1909 by The Macmillan Company, new revised and enlarged edition, copyright 1954 by The Macmillan Company; "Yankee Cradle" from *Selected Poems* by Robert P. Tristram Coffin,

ACKNOWLEDGMENTS

copyright 1929, 1932, 1933, 1935, 1937, 1938, 1939, 1942, 1943, 1945 by The Macmillan Company; all used by permission of The Macmillan Company.

THE MACMILLAN COMPANY OF CANADA LTD., THE AUTHOR'S REPRESENTATIVES and MACMILLAN & COMPANY LTD. for permission to reprint "The Yarn of the *Nancy Belle*" and "Captain Reece" from *Bab Ballads* by W. S. Gilbert in the Dominion of Canada.

THE MACMILLAN COMPANY OF CANADA LTD., THE TRUSTEES OF THE HARDY ESTATE and MACMILLAN & COMPANY LTD. for permission to reprint "Weathers" and "The Darkling Thrush" from *Collected Poems of Thomas Hardy* in the Dominion of Canada.

THE MACMILLAN COMPANY OF CANADA LTD., MRS. STEPHENS and MACMILLAN & COMPANY LTD. for permission to reprint "Seumas Beg" from *Collected Poems* by James Stephens in the Dominion of Canada.

JOHN MURRAY for permission to reprint "A Subaltern's Love-Song" and "Trebetherick" from *John Betjeman's Collected Poems*, published by Houghton Mifflin Company and John Murray, in the Dominion of Canada.

NEW DIRECTIONS for "Fern Hill" from *The Collected Poems of Dylan Thomas*, copyright 1952, 1953 by Dylan Thomas; "Spring and All" from *The Collected Earlier Poems of William Carlos Williams*, copyright 1938, 1951 by William Carlos Williams; "Anthem for Doomed Youth" from *The Poems of Wilfred Owen*, all rights reserved; all reprinted by permission of New Directions.

PENGUIN BOOKS LTD. for "The Owl-Critic" by J. T. Fields from *The Penguin Book of Comic and Curious Verse*, ed. J. M. Cohen.

A. D. PETERS for permission to reprint "Jim, Who ran away from his Nurse and Was Eaten by a Lion," "The Python" and "The Llama" from *Cautionary Verses* by Hilaire Belloc, published by Gerald Duckworth and Company Ltd., in the Dominion of Canada.

G. P. PUTNAM'S SONS for "We Have Been Here Before" from *Spilt Milk* by Morris Bishop, copyright © 1942 by Morris Bishop; "Our Silly Little Sister" from *All Together* by Dorothy Aldis; all used by permission of G. P. Putnam's Sons, publishers.

THE RICHARD PRESS LTD. for "A Runnable Stag" by John Davidson.

CHARLES SCRIBNER'S SONS for "The Whole Duty of Children" and "The Land of Counterpane" from *A Child's Garden of Verses* by Robert Louis Stevenson, Scribner Illustrated Classics Edition; both used by permission of Charles Scribner's Sons.

MARTIN SECKER & WARBURG LTD. and THE AUTHOR'S EXECUTRIX for "The Old Ships" by James Elroy Flecker.

ACKNOWLEDGMENTS

THE SOCIETY OF AUTHORS AS THE LITERARY REPRESENTA-TIVE OF THE ESTATE OF MISS ROSE FYLEMAN for permission to reprint "Mice" from Rose Fyleman's *Fifty-One Nursery Rhymes* in the Dominion of Canada.

THE SOCIETY OF AUTHORS AS THE REPRESENTATIVE OF THE LITERARY TRUSTEES OF WALTER DE LA MARE for "The Little Creature" from Walter de la Mare's *Poems;* "Alas, Alack" and "The Bandog" from Walter de la Mare's *Peacock Pie;* "The Little Green Orchard" from Walter de la Mare's *Down-Adown-Derry.*

THE SOCIETY OF AUTHORS AS THE LITERARY REPRESENTA-TIVE OF THE ESTATE OF THE LATE A. E. HOUSMAN AND MESSRS. JONATHAN CAPE LTD., publishers of A. E. Housman's *Collected Poems*, for permission to reprint two verses from A. E. Housman's *A Shropshire Lad* in the Dominion of Canada.

NANCY BYRD TURNER for "Old Quin Queeribus" from *Zodiac Town,* published by Little, Brown and Company.

A. P. WATT & SON AND THE AUTHOR for "1805" and "Lollocks" from *Collected Poems* by Robert Graves, published by Doubleday & Company, Inc., and by Cassell & Co., Ltd.

A. P. WATT & SON, MRS. BAMBRIDGE AND THE MACMILLAN COMPANY OF CANADA LTD. for permission to reprint "The Looking-Glass" from *Rewards and Fairies* by Rudyard Kipling and "The Camel's Hump" from *Just-So Stories* by Rudyard Kipling in the Dominion of Canada.

A. P. WATT AND SON, SIR ALAN HERBERT, THE PROPRIETORS OF *PUNCH* AND THE PUBLISHERS, ERNEST BENN LTD. for "The Prodigy" from *A Book of Ballads* by A. P. Herbert, copyright © 1925 by *Punch*.

A. P. WATT AND SON, MISS D. E. COLLINS AND MESSRS. ME-THUEN & CO. LTD. for permission to reprint "The Rolling English Road" and "Elegy in a Country Churchyard" from *Collected Poems of G. K. Chesterton* in the Dominion of Canada.

Foreword

In my youth I was fond of a rousing and innocent musical-comedy song called "Everybody Ought to Know How to Do the Tickletoe." The tune and the title still cheerfully haunt me. At one time they were the basis for a game with which I used to harass my children, interrupting their pleasures to remark, for example, that although a knowledge of spinning or needlepoint was useful to many, there was one thing that everybody ought to know. Their dutiful "What is that, Daddy?" left them wide open, of course, to the triumphant reply, "How to do the tickletoe." By ingeniously rephrasing the come-on I was

9

able to elicit an occasional further "What is that, Daddy?," but they grew wary, and progressively harder to trap. I had to resort to progressively sneakier stratagems. The finish came the day they were caught off guard when asked if they had heard the latest news about Howdy Doody, whom they detested. Hoping he had broken his neck, they took the bait. On being informed that everybody ought to know Howdy Doody tickletoe, they got married and moved away.

Happily there are other things than the tickletoe that everybody ought to know, and among them are the poems, verses and jingles in this book. Many of you already know some of them, and some of you know many of them. I should like all of you to know all of them, because when you do you will have had at least a sparrow's-eye view of a kingdom awaiting your closer exploration, in whose heights lie treasures more precious than the gold of El Dorado, and in whose depths, rewards as serviceable as the borax of Death Valley. There is good stuff in the middle, too.

One word of warning before you start. Great names make news, but great names do not necessarily make great poems. You will find here great poems by famous poets, great poems by obscure poets, and some of the greatest poems by nameless poets. You will also find some ludicrously bad poems by obscure poets and a few equally excruciating by poets who monopolize the pages of the *Oxford Book of English Verse*. As you must have discovered by now, I have a tiresome sense of humor, so I shall not force upon you my opinion of what is good and what is bad. Your own taste must be your Geiger counter. Happy prospecting!

Ogden Nash

Everybody Ought to Know

HUNTING SONG

Sir Walter Scott

Waken, lords and ladies gay,
On the mountain dawns the day,
All the jolly chase is here,
With horse, and hawk, and hunting spear!
Hounds are in their couples yelling,
Hawks are whistling, horns are knelling.
Merrily, merrily, mingle they,
"Waken, lords and ladies gay."

Waken, lords and ladies gay,
The mist has left the mountain grey,
Springlets in the dawn are steaming,
Diamonds on the brake are gleaming,
And foresters have busy been
To track the buck in thicket green;
Now we come to chant our lay,
"Waken, lords and ladies gay."

Waken, lords and ladies gay,
To the greenwood haste away;
We can show you where he lies,
Fleet of foot, and tall of size;
We can show the marks he made
When 'gainst oak his antlers frayed;
You shall see him brought to bay;
"Waken, lords and ladies gay."

Louder, louder chant the lay,
Waken, lords and ladies gay!

Tell them youth, and mirth, and glee,
Run a course as well as we;
Time, stern huntsman! who can baulk,
Stanch as hound, and fleet as hawk?
Think of this, and rise with day,
Gentle lords and ladies gay!

THE ROAD NOT TAKEN

Robert Frost

Two roads diverged in a yellow wood,
And sorry I could not travel both
And be one traveler, long I stood
And looked down one as far as I could
To where it bent in the undergrowth;

Then took the other, as just as fair,
And having perhaps the better claim,
Because it was grassy and wanted wear;
Though as for that the passing there
Had worn them really about the same,

And both that morning equally lay
In leaves no step had trodden black.
Oh, I kept the first for another day!
Yet knowing how way leads on to way,
I doubted if I should ever come back.

I shall be telling this with a sigh
Somewhere ages and ages hence:

14

Two roads diverged in a wood, and I—
I took the one less traveled by,
And that has made all the difference.

TO DAFFODILS
Robert Herrick

Fair daffodils, we weep to see
    You haste away so soon;
As yet the early-rising sun
    Has not attain'd his noon.
        Stay, stay
    Until the hasting day
        Has run
    But to the evensong;
And, having pray'd together, we
    Will go with you along.

We have short time to stay, as you,
    We have as short a spring;
As quick a growth to meet decay,
    As you, or anything.
        We die
    As your hours do, and dry
        Away
    Like to the summer's rain;
Or as the pearls of morning's dew,
    Ne'er to be found again.

THE ROLLING ENGLISH ROAD

G. K. Chesterton

Before the Roman came to Rye or out to Severn strode,
The rolling English drunkard made the rolling English road.
A reeling road, a rolling road, that rambles round the shire,
And after him the parson ran, the sexton and the squire;
A merry road, a mazy road, and such as we did tread
The night we went to Birmingham by way of Beachy Head.

I knew no harm of Bonaparte and plenty of the Squire,
And for to fight the Frenchman I did not much desire;
But I did bash their baggonets because they came arrayed
To straighten out the crooked road an English drunkard
     made,
Where you and I went down the lane with ale-mugs in our
     hands,
The night we went to Glastonbury by way of Goodwin Sands.

16

His sins they were forgiven him; or why do flowers run
Behind him; and the hedges all strengthening in the sun?
The wild thing went from left to right and knew not which
      was which,
But the wild rose was above him when they found him in the
      ditch.
God pardon us, nor harden us; we did not see so clear
The night we went to Bannockburn by way of Brighton Pier.

My friends, we will not go again or ape an ancient rage,
Or stretch the folly of our youth to be the shame of age,
But walk with clearer eyes and ears this path that
      wandereth,
And see undrugged in evening light the decent inn of death;
For there is good news yet to hear and fine things to be seen,
Before we go to Paradise by way of Kensal Green.

1805

Robert Graves

At Viscount Nelson's lavish funeral,
    While the mob milled and yelled about St. Paul's,
A General chatted with an Admiral:

'One of your Colleagues, Sir, remarked today
    That Nelson's *exit*, though to be lamented,
Falls not inopportunely, in its way.'

'He was a thorn in our flesh,' came the reply—
    'The most bird-witted, unaccountable,
Odd little runt that ever I did spy.

'One arm, one peeper, vain as Pretty Poll,
    A meddler, too, in foreign politics
And gave his heart in pawn to a plain moll.

'He would dare lecture us Sea Lords, and then
    Would treat his ratings as though men of honour
And play at leap-frog with his midshipmen!

'We tried to box him down, but up he popped,
    And when he'd banged Napoleon at the Nile
Became too much the hero to be dropped.

'You've heard that Copenhagen "blind eye" story?
    We'd tied him to Nurse Parker's apron-strings—
By G–d, he snipped them through and snatched the glory!'

'Yet,' cried the General, 'six-and-twenty sail
    Captured or sunk by him off Tráfalgár—
That writes a handsome *finis* to the tale.'

'Handsome enough. The seas are England's now.
    That fellow's foibles need no longer plague us.
He died most creditably, I'll allow.'

'And, Sir, the secret of his victories?'
    'By his unServicelike, familiar ways, Sir,
He made the whole Fleet love him, damn his eyes!'

18

SNEEZE ON A MONDAY . . .

Author Unknown

Sneeze on a Monday, you sneeze for danger;
Sneeze on a Tuesday, you'll kiss a stranger;
Sneeze on a Wednesday, you sneeze for a letter;
Sneeze on a Thursday, for something better;
Sneeze on a Friday, you sneeze for sorrow;
Sneeze on a Saturday, your sweetheart to-morrow;
Sneeze on a Sunday, your safety seek—
The devil will have you the whole of the week.

GUESTS

Author Unknown

Yet if His Majesty, our sovereign lord,
Should of his own accord
Friendly himself invite,
And say, 'I'll be your guest to-morrow night,'
How should we stir ourselves, call and command
All hands to work! 'Let no man idle stand!

'Set me fine Spanish tables in the hall;
See they be fitted all;
Let there be room to eat
And order taken that there want no meat.
See every sconce and candlestick made bright,
That without tapers they may give a light.

'Look to the presence: are the carpets spread,
The dazie o'er the head,
The cushions in the chairs,
And all the candles lighted on the stairs?
Perfume the chambers, and in any case
Let each man give attendance in his place!'

Thus, if a king were coming, would we do;
And 'twere good reason too;
For 'tis a duteous thing
To show all honour to an earthly king,
And after all our travail and our cost,
So he be pleased, to think no labour lost.

But at the coming of the King of Heaven
All's set at six and seven;
We wallow in our sin,
Christ cannot find a chamber in the inn.
We entertain Him always like a stranger,
And, as at first, still lodge Him in the manger.

OLD MEN

Ogden Nash

People expect old men to die,
They do not really mourn old men.
Old men are different. People look
At them with eyes that wonder when . . .
People watch with unshocked eyes;
But the old men know when an old man dies.

20

HERE LIES A LADY
John Crowe Ransom

Here lies a lady of beauty and high degree.
Of chills and fever she died, of fever and chills,
The delight of her husband, her aunts, an infant of three,
And of medicos marveling sweetly on her ills.

For either she burned, and her confident eyes would blaze,
And her fingers fly in a manner to puzzle their heads—
What was she making? Why, nothing; she sat in a maze
Of old scraps of laces, snipped into curious shreds—

Or this would pass, and the light of her fire decline
Till she lay discouraged and cold as a thin stalk white
        and blown,
And would not open her eyes, to kisses, to wine.
The sixth of these states was her last; the cold settled down.

Sweet ladies, long may ye bloom, and toughly I hope ye
        may thole,
But was she not lucky? In flowers and lace and mourning,
In love and great honor we bade God rest her soul
After six little spaces of chill, and six of burning.

THE RUM TUM TUGGER
T. S. Eliot

The Rum Tum Tugger is a Curious Cat:
If you offer him pheasant he would rather have grouse.

If you put him in a house he would much prefer a flat,
If you put him in a flat then he'd rather have a house.
If you set him on a mouse then he only wants a rat,
If you set him on a rat then he'd rather chase a mouse.
Yes the Rum Tum Tugger is a Curious Cat—
    And there isn't any call for me to shout it:
        For he will do
        As he do do
            And there's no doing anything about it!

22

The Rum Tum Tugger is a terrible bore:
When you let him in, then he wants to be out;
He's always on the wrong side of every door,
And as soon as he's at home, then he'd like to get about.
He likes to lie in the bureau drawer,
But he makes such a fuss if he can't get out.
Yes the Rum Tum Tugger is a Curious Cat—
 And it isn't any use for you to doubt it:
  For he will do
  As he do do
   And there's no doing anything about it!

 The Rum Tum Tugger is a curious beast:
His disobliging ways are a matter of habit.
If you offer him fish than he always wants a feast;
When there isn't any fish then he won't eat rabbit.
If you offer him cream then he sniffs and sneers,
For he only likes what he finds for himself;
So you'll catch him in it right up to the ears,
If you put it away on the larder shelf.
The Rum Tum Tugger is artful and knowing,
The Rum Tum Tugger doesn't care for a cuddle;
But he'll leap on your lap in the middle of your sewing,
For there's nothing he enjoys like a horrible muddle.
Yes the Rum Tum Tugger is a Curious Cat—
 And there isn't any need for me to spout it:
  For he will do
  As he do do
   And there's no doing anything about it!

THE WITCH'S BALLAD

William Bell Scott

O I hae come from far away,
 From a warm land far away,
A southern land across the sea,
With sailor-lads about the mast,
Merry and canny, and kind to me.

And I hae been to yon town
 To try my luck in yon town;
Nort, and Mysie, Elspie too.
Right braw we were to pass the gate,
Wi' gowden clasps on girdles blue.

Mysie smiled wi' miminy [1] mouth,
 Innocent mouth, miminy mouth;
Elspie wore a scarlet gown,
Nort's grey eyes were unco' gleg.[2]
My Castile comb was like a crown.

We walk'd abreast all up the street,
 Into the market, up the street;
Our hair with marigolds was wound,
Our bodices with love-knots laced,
Our merchandise with tansy bound.

Nort had chickens, I had cocks,
 Gamesome cocks, loud-crowing cocks;
Mysie ducks, and Elspie drakes,—
For a wee groat or a pound;
We lost nae time wi' gives and takes.

—Lost nae time, for well we knew,
    In our sleeves full well we knew,
When the gloaming came that night,
Duck nor drake, nor hen nor cock
Would be found by candle-light.

And when our chaffering all was done,
    All was paid for, sold and done,
We drew a glove on ilka hand,
We sweetly curtsied, each to each,
And deftly danced a saraband.

The market-lassies look'd and laugh'd,
    Left their gear, and look'd and laugh'd;
They made as they would join the game,
But soon their mithers, wild and wud,[3]
With whack and screech they stopp'd the same.

Sae loud the tongues o' randies[4] grew,
    The flytin'[5] and the skirlin'[6] grew,
At all the windows in the place,
Wi' spoons or knives, wi' needle or awl,
Was thrust out every hand and face.

And down each stair they throng'd anon,
    Gentle, semple, throng'd anon:
Souter[7] and tailor, frowsy Nan,
The ancient widow young again,
 Simpering behind her fan.

---

[1] miminy/prim, demure   [2] gleg/bright, sharp   [3] wud/mad
[4] randies/viragoes   [5] flytin'/scolding   [6] skirlin'/shrieking
[7] souter/cobbler

Without a choice, against their will,
    Doited, [8] dazed, against their will,
The market lassie and her mither,
The farmer and his husbandman,
Hand in hand dance a' thegither.

Slow at first, but faster soon,
    Still increasing, wild and fast,
Hoods and mantles, hats and hose,
Blindly doff'd and cast away,
Left them naked, heads and toes.

They would have torn us limb from limb,
    Dainty limb from dainty limb;
But never one of them could win
Across the line that I had drawn
With bleeding thumb a-widdershin.[9]

But there was Jeff the provost's son,
    Jeff the provost's only son;
There was Father Auld himsel',
The Lombard frae the hostelry,
And the lawyer Peter Fell.

All goodly men we singled out,
    Waled [10] them well, and singled out,
And drew them by the left hand in;
Mysie the priest, and Elspie won
The Lombard, Nort the lawyer carle,
I mysel' the provost's son.

[8] doited/mazed   [9] a-widdershin/the wrong way of the sun: or E. to W.
through N.   [10] waled/chose

26

Then, with cantrip [11] kisses seven,
 Three times round with kisses seven,
Warp'd and woven there spun we
Arms and legs and flaming hair,
Like a whirlwind on the sea.

Like a wind that sucks the sea,
 Over and in and on the sea,
Good sooth it was a mad delight;
And every man of all the four
Shut his eyes and laugh'd outright.

Laugh'd as long as they had breath,
 Laugh'd while they had sense or breath;
And close about us coil'd a mist
Of gnats and midges, wasps and flies,
Like the whirlwind shaft it rist.

Drawn up I was right off my feet,
 Into the mist and off my feet;
And, dancing on each chimney-top,
I saw a thousand darling imps
Keeping time with skip and hop.

And on the provost's brave ridge-tile,
 On the provost's grand ridge-tile,
The Blackamoor first to master me
I saw, I saw that winsome smile,
The mouth that did my heart beguile,
And spoke the great Word over me,
In the land beyond the sea.

[11] cantrip/magic

I call'd his name, I call'd aloud,
    Alas! I call'd on him aloud;
And then he filled his hand with stour,[12]
And threw it towards me in the air;
My mouse flew out, I lost my pow'r!

My lusty strength, my power were gone;
    Power was gone, and all was gone.
He will not let me love him more!
Of bell and whip and horse's tail
He cares not if I find a store.

But I am proud if he is fierce!
    I am proud as he is fierce;
I'll turn about and backward go,
If I meet again that Blackamoor,
And he'll help us then, for he shall know
I seek another paramour.

And we'll gang once more to yon town,
    Wi' better luck to yon town;
We'll walk in silk and cramoisie,[13]
And I shall wed the provost's son
My lady of the town I'll be!

For I was born a crown'd king's child,
    Born and nursed a king's child,
King o' a land ayont [14] the sea,
Where the Blackamoor kiss'd me first,
And taught me art and glamourie.[15]

---

[12] stour/dust   [13] cramoisie/crimson   [14] ayont/beyond
[15] glamourie/wizardry

28

Each one in her wame shall hide
    Her hairy mouse, her wary mouse,
Fed on madwort and agramie,—
Wear amber beads between her breasts,
And blind-worm's skin about her knee.

The Lombard shall be Elspie's man,
    Elspie's gowden husband-man;
Nort shall take the lawyer's hand;
The priest shall swear another vow:
We'll dance again the saraband!

FATE IS UNFAIR

Don Marquis

in many places here and
there
i think that fate
is quite unfair
yon centipede upon
the floor
can boast of
tootsies by the score
consider my
distressing fix
my feet are limited to six
did i a hundred
feet possess

29

would all that glorious
footfulness
enable me
to stagger less
when i am
overcome by heat
or if i had
a hundred feet
would i
careering oer the floor
stagger
proportionately more
well i suppose
the mind serene
will not tell
destiny its mean
the truly
philosophic mind
will use
such feet as it can find
and follow calmly
fast or slow
the feet it has
where eer they go
                    archy

"Tick - le   ick - le   tick - le

MICE

Rose Fyleman

I think mice
Are rather nice.

> Their tails are long,
> Their faces small,
> They haven't any
> Chins at all.
> Their ears are pink,
> Their teeth are white,
> They run about
> The house at night.
> They nibble things
> They shouldn't touch
> And no one seems
> To like them much.

But *I* think mice
Are nice.

31

THE MERRY MONTH OF MARCH

William Wordsworth

The cock is crowing,
The stream is flowing,
The small birds twitter,
The lake doth glitter,
The green field sleeps in the sun;
The oldest and youngest
Are at work with the strongest;
The cattle are grazing,
Their heads never raising;
There are forty feeding like one!
Like an army defeated
The snow hath retreated,
And now doth fare ill
On the top of the bare hill;
The Plough-boy is whooping anon, anon.
There's joy in the mountains;
There's life in the fountains;
Small clouds are sailing,
Blue sky prevailing;
The rain is over and gone!

JERUSALEM   *from Milton*

William Blake

And did those feet in ancient time
Walk upon England's mountains green?
And was the holy Lamb of God
On England's pleasant pastures seen?

32

And did the countenance divine
Shine forth upon our clouded hills?
And was Jerusalem builded here
Among these dark Satanic mills?

Bring me my bow of burning gold!
Bring me my arrows of desire!
Bring me my spear! O clouds, unfold!
Bring me my chariot of fire!

I will not cease from mental fight,
Nor shall my sword sleep in my hand,
Till we have built Jerusalem
In England's green and pleasant land.

THE WRAGGLE TAGGLE GIPSIES

Author Unknown

There were three gipsies a-come to my door,
And downstairs ran this a-lady, O!
One sang high, and another sang low,
And the other sang, Bonny, bonny Biscay, O!

Then she pulled off her silk-finished gown
And put on hose of leather, O!
The ragged, ragged rags about our door—
She's gone with the wraggle taggle gipsies, O!

It was late last night, when my lord came home,
Enquiring for his a-lady, O!
The servants said, on every hand:
"She's gone with the wraggle taggle gipsies, O!"

"O saddle to me my milk-white steed.
Go and fetch me my pony, O!
That I may ride and seek my bride,
Who is gone with the wraggle taggle gipsies, O!"

O he rode high and he rode low,
He rode through woods and copses too,
Until he came to an open field,
And there he espied his a-lady, O!

"What makes you leave your house and land?
What makes you leave your money, O?

34

What makes you leave your new-wedded lord;
To go with the wraggle taggle gipsies, O!"

"What care I for my house and my land?
What care I for my money, O?
What care I for my new-wedded lord?
I'm off with the wraggle taggle gipsies, O!"

"Last night you slept on a goose-feather bed,
With the sheet turned down so bravely, O!
And to-night you'll sleep in a cold open field,
Along with the wraggle taggle gipsies, O!"

"What care I for a goose-feather bed,
With the sheet turned down so bravely, O?
For to-night I shall sleep in a cold open field,
Along with the wraggle taggle gipsies, O!"

CAPE ANN

T. S. Eliot

O quick quick quick, quick hear the song-sparrow,
Swamp-sparrow, fox-sparrow, vesper-sparrow
At dawn and dusk. Follow the dance
Of the goldfinch at noon. Leave to chance
The Blackburnian Warbler, the shy one. Hail
With shrill whistle the note of the quail, the bob-white
Dodging by bay-bush. Follow the feet
Of the walker, the water-thrush. Follow the flight
Of the dancing arrow, the purple martin. Greet

In silence the bullbat. All are delectable. Sweet sweet sweet
But resign this land at the end, resign it
To its true owner, the tough one, the sea-gull.
The palaver is finished.

THE FAIRIES

William Allingham

Up the airy mountain,
    Down the rushy glen,
We daren't go a-hunting
    For fear of little men;
Wee folk, good folk,
    Trooping all together;
Green jacket, red cap,
    And white owl's feather!

Down along the rocky shore
    Some make their home,
They live on crispy pancakes
    Of yellow tide-foam;
Some in the reeds
    Of the black mountain lake,
With frogs for their watch-dogs,
    All night awake.

High on the hill-top
    The old King sits;
He is now so old and grey
    He's nigh lost his wits.

With a bridge of white mist
    Columbkill he crosses,
On his stately journeys
    From Slieveleague to Rosses;
Or going up with music
    On cold starry nights,
To sup with the Queen
    Of the gay Northern Lights.

They stole little Bridget
    For seven years long;
When she came down again
    Her friends were all gone.
They took her lightly back,
    Between the night and morrow,
They thought that she was fast asleep,
    But she was dead with sorrow.
They have kept her ever since
    Deep within the lake,
On a bed of flag-leaves,
    Watching till she wake.

By the craggy hill-side,
    Through the mosses bare,
They have planted thorn-trees
    For pleasure here and there.
Is any man so daring
    As dig them up in spite,
He shall find their sharpest thorns
    In his bed at night.

Up the airy mountain,
    Down the rushy glen,

We daren't go a-hunting
    For fear of little men;
Wee folk, good folk,
    Trooping all together;
Green jacket, red cap,
    And white owl's feather!

THE MAN FROM PORLOCK

Helen Bevington

The man knocked strongly at the door
And listened for the step within,
Then pounded louder than before.
Either the fellow was not in,

Or must be loony, or asleep.
But Porlock was a goodish way
And rocky lay the path and steep.
A man had work to do that day.

He pushed the latch, revealing where
The fellow sat, awake and still,
And scrawled upon a paper there.
The man from Porlock took it ill.

He cried his errand. Silently
The other heard and dropped his pen
And bore the tale, while fretfully
The man recited it again.

The man from Porlock left the place
To do the work he had to do.
And fear was on the other's face,
Who had returned from Xanadu.

And fear was in the other's eyes,
For he on honey-dew had fed
And drunk the milk of Paradise.
And now the song was quieted.

THE VOICE OF THE LOBSTER

Lewis Carroll

'Tis the voice of the Lobster; I heard him declare,
"You have baked me too brown, I must sugar my hair."
As a duck with his eyelids, so he with his nose
Trims his belt and his buttons, and turns out his toes.
When the sands are all dry, he is gay as a lark,
And will talk in contemptuous tones of the Shark:
But, when the tide rises and sharks are around,
His voice has a timid and tremulous sound.

I passed by his garden, and marked, with one eye,
How the Owl and the Panther were sharing a pie:
The Panther took pie-crust, and gravy, and meat,
While the Owl had the dish as its share of the treat.
When the pie was all finished, the Owl, as a boon,
Was kindly permitted to pocket the spoon:
While the Panther received knife and fork with a growl,
And concluded the banquet by——

WHAT YOU WILL LEARN ABOUT THE BROBINYAK

John Ciardi

The Brobinyak has Dragon Eyes
And a tail the shape of a Fern
And teeth about Banana Size,
As one day you may learn
If you ever sail across the Sea
On the Shell of a Giant Clam
And come to the Forest of Foofenzee
In the Land of the Pshah of Psham.

There is no language he can't speak
And you may, if you please,
Be swallowed whole in French or Greek,
Or nibbled in Chinese.

And once inside the Brobinyak
You'll meet a lot of friends:
The Three-Toed Gleep and the Saginsack
And a covey of Two-Tailed Bends.

The Russian Bear is always there,
    And Glocks from the Polar Sea.
And Radio Eels with static squeals,
    And the Piebald Peccary.
The Splinterwave from his Ocean Cave
    Will greet you at the door.
The Green Kilkenny collect your penny
    And pitch it along the floor.

The Banjo Tern and the Fiddling Hern
        Will play you a Wedding March.
But keep your eye on the Lullaby
        Or he'll nibble your collar for starch.
Oh keep your eye on the Lullaby
        And never speak to the Mullet,
Or the Scrawny Shank will leave his Tank
        And nibble you quick as a bullet.
And never look at the Seven-Nosed Hook
        Or, with a frightful roar,
He'll sniff enough of his Pepper Snuff
        To sneeze you out the door.

Oh the Brobinyak has Dragon Eyes
And a tail the shape of a Fern
And teeth about Banana Size,
As one day you may learn
If ever you sail across the Sea
On the Shell of a Giant Clam
And come to the Forest of Foofenzee
In the Land of the Pshah of Psham.

A MAN SAW A BALL OF GOLD IN THE SKY

Stephen Crane

A man saw a ball of gold in the sky;
He climbed for it,
And eventually achieved it—
It was clay.

41

Now this is the strange part:
When this man went to the earth
And looked again,
Lo, there was the ball of gold.
Now this is the strange part:
It was a ball of gold.
Ay, by the heavens, it was a ball of gold.

WEATHERS

Thomas Hardy

I

This is the weather the cuckoo likes,
　　And so do I;
When showers betumble the chestnut spikes,
　　And nestlings fly:
And the little brown nightingale bills his best,
　　And they sit outside at "The Travellers' Rest,"
And maids come forth sprig-muslin drest,
And citizens dream of the south and west,
　　And so do I.

II

This is the weather the shepherd shuns,
　　And so do I;
When beeches drip in browns and duns,
　　And thresh, and ply;

42

And hill-hid tides throb, throe on throe,
And meadow rivulets overflow,
And drops on gate-bars hang in a row,
And rooks in families homeward go,
    And so do I.

ARIEL'S DIRGE

William Shakespeare

Full fathom five thy father lies;
    Of his bones are coral made;
Those are pearls that were his eyes:
Nothing of him that doth fade,
But doth suffer a sea-change
Into something rich and strange.
Sea-nymphs hourly ring his knell:
    Ding-dong.
Hark! now I hear them,—
    Ding-dong, bell!

A NOISELESS PATIENT SPIDER

Walt Whitman

A noiseless patient spider,
I mark'd where on a little promontory it stood isolated,
Mark'd how to explore the vacant vast surrounding,
It launched forth filament, filament, filament, out of itself,
Ever unreeling them, ever tirelessly speeding them.
And you O my soul where you stand,
Surrounded, detached, in measureless oceans of space,
Ceaselessly musing, venturing, throwing, seeking the spheres
        to connect them,
Till the bridge you will need be form'd, till the ductile
        anchor hold,
Till the gossamer thread you fling catch somewhere, O my
        soul.

44

FERN HILL

Dylan Thomas

Now as I was young and easy under the apple boughs
About the lilting house and happy as the grass was green,
    The night above the dingle starry,
        Time let me hail and climb
      Golden in the heydays of his eyes,
And honoured among wagons I was prince of the apple
              towns
And once below a time I lordly had the trees and leaves
        Trail with daisies and barley
      Down the rivers of the windfall light.

And as I was green and carefree, famous among the barns
About the happy yard and singing as the farm was home,
    In the sun that is young once only,
        Time let me play and be
      Golden in the mercy of his means,
And green and golden I was huntsman and herdsman, the
              calves
Sang to my horn, the foxes on the hills barked clear and
              cold,
        And the sabbath rang slowly
      In the pebbles of the holy streams.

All the sun long it was running, it was lovely, the hay
Fields high as the house, the tunes from the chimneys, it
              was air
    And playing, lovely and watery
        And fire green as grass.
      And nightly under the simple stars

45

As I rode to sleep the owls were bearing the farm away,
All the moon long I heard, blessed among stables, the night
            jars
      Flying with the ricks, and the horses
            Flashing into the dark.

And then to awake, and the farm, like a wanderer white
With the dew, come back, the cock on his shoulder: it
            was all
      Shining, it was Adam and maiden,
            The sky gathered again
      And the sun grew round that very day.
So it must have been after the birth of the simple light
In the first, spinning place, the spellbound horses walking
            warm
      Out of the whinnying green stable
            On to the fields of praise.

And honoured among foxes and pheasants by the gay house
Under the new made clouds and happy as the heart was
            long,
      In the sun born over and over,
            I ran my heedless ways,
      My wishes raced through the house high hay
And nothing I cared, at my sky blue trades, that time allows
In all his tuneful turning so few and such morning songs
      Before the children green and golden
            Follow him out of grace,

Nothing I cared, in the lamb white days, that time would
            take me
Up to the swallow thronged loft by the shadow of my hand,
46

In the moon that is always rising,
    Nor that riding to sleep
I should hear him fly with the high fields
And wake to the farm forever fled from the childless land.
Oh as I was young and easy in the mercy of his means,
    Time held me green and dying
Though I sang in my chains like the sea.

GOING BACK AGAIN

Robert Lytton

I dream'd that I walk'd in Italy,
    When the day was going down,
By a water that silently wander'd by
    Thro' an old dim-lighted town,

Till I came to a palace fair to see.
    Wide open the windows were
My love at a window sat; and she
    Beckon'd me up the stair. . . .

When I came to the little rose-colour'd room,
    From the curtains out flew a bat.
The window was open: and in the gloom
    My love at the window sat.

She sat with her guitar on her knee,
    But she was not singing a note,
For someone had drawn (ah, who could it be?)
    A knife across her throat.

THE OLD BUCCANEER

Charles Kingsley

Oh England is a pleasant place for them that's rich and
      high,
But England is a cruel place for such poor folks as I;
And such a port for mariners I ne'er shall see again
As the pleasant Isle of Avès, beside the Spanish main.

There were forty craft in Avès that were both swift and
      stout,
All furnished well with small arms and cannon round
      about;
And a thousand men in Avès made laws so fair and free
To choose their valiant captains and obey them loyally.

Thence we sailed against the Spaniard with his hoards
      of plate and gold,
Which he wrung with cruel tortures from Indian folk
      of old;
Likewise the merchant captains, with hearts as hard as
      stone,
Who flog men, and keel-haul them, and starve them to
      the bone.

O the palms grew high in Avès, and fruits that shone like
      gold,
And the colibris [1] and parrots they were gorgeous to
      behold;
And the negro maids to Avès from bondage fast did flee,
To welcome gallant sailors, a-sweeping in from sea.

48

O sweet it was in Avès to hear the landward breeze,
A-swing with good tobacco in a net between the trees,
With a negro lass to fan you, while you listened to the roar
Of the breakers on the reef outside, that never touched
        the shore.

But Scripture saith, an ending to all fine things must be;
So the King's ships sailed on Avès, and quite put down
        were we.
All day we fought like bulldogs, but they burst the booms
        at night;
And I fled in a piragua,[2] sore wounded, from the fight.

Nine days I floated starving, and a negro lass beside,
Till, for all I tried to cheer her, the poor young thing
        she died;
But as I lay a-gasping, a Bristol sail came by,
And brought me home to England here, to beg until I die.

And now I'm old and going—I'm sure I can't tell where;
One comfort is, this world's so hard, I can't be worse
        off there:
If I might be a sea-dove, I'd fly across the main,
To the pleasant Isle of Avès, to look at it once again.

[1] colibris/humming-birds   [2] piragua/dug-out canoe

THE DESTRUCTION OF SENNACHERIB

George Gordon, Lord Byron

The Assyrian came down like the wolf on the fold,
And his cohorts were gleaming in purple and gold;
And the sheen of their spears was like stars on the sea,
When the blue wave rolls nightly on deep Galilee.

Like the leaves of the forest when Summer is green,
That host with their banners at sunset were seen:
Like the leaves of the forest when Autumn hath blown,
That host on the morrow lay wither'd and strown.

For the Angel of Death spread his wings on the blast,
And breathed in the face of the foe as he passed;
And the eyes of the sleepers waxed deadly and chill,
And their hearts but once heaved, and for ever grew still!

And there lay the steed with his nostril all wide,
But through it there rolled not the breath of his pride;
And the foam of his gasping lay white on the turf,
And cold as the spray of the rock-beating surf.

And there lay the rider distorted and pale,
With the dew on his brow, and the rust on his mail;
And the tents were all silent, the banners alone,
The lances unlifted, the trumpet unblown.

And the widows of Ashur are loud in their wail,
And the idols are broken in the temple of Baal;
And the might of the Gentile, unsmote by the sword,
Hath melted like snow in the glance of the Lord!

From *THE THORN*

William Wordsworth

And they had fixed the wedding day,
The morning that must wed them both;
But Stephen to another Maid
Had sworn another oath;
And with this other Maid, to church
Unthinking Stephen went—
Poor Martha! on that woeful day
A cruel, cruel fire, they say,
Into her bones was sent:
It dried her body like a cinder,
And almost turned her brain to tinder.

THE TURNIP SELLER

Samuel Johnson

If a man who turnips cries,
Cry not when his father dies,
It is proof that he would rather
Have a turnip than his father.

THE GARDENER'S SONG

Lewis Carroll

He thought he saw an Elephant,
    That practised on a fife:
He looked again, and found it was
    A letter from his wife.
"At length I realise," he said,
    "The bitterness of life!"

He thought he saw a Buffalo
    Upon the chimney-piece:
He looked again, and found it was
    His Sister's Husband's Niece.
"Unless you leave this house," he said,
    "I'll send for the Police!"

He thought he saw a Rattlesnake
    That questioned him in Greek:
He looked again, and found it was
    The Middle of Next Week.
"The one thing I regret," he said,
    "Is that it cannot speak!"

52

He thought he saw a Banker's Clerk
    Descending from the 'bus:
He looked again, and found it was
    A Hippopotamus.
"If this should stay to dine," he said,
    "There won't be much for us!"

He thought he saw a Kangaroo
    That worked a coffee-mill:
He looked again, and found it was
    A Vegetable-Pill.
"Were I to swallow this," he said,
    "I should be very ill!"

He thought he saw a Coach-and-Four
    That stood beside his bed:
He looked again, and found it was
    A Bear without a Head.
"Poor thing," he said, "poor silly thing!
    It's waiting to be fed!"

He thought he saw an Albatross
    That fluttered round the lamp:
He looked again, and found it was
    A Penny-Postage-Stamp.
"You'd best be getting home," he said:
    "The nights are very damp!"

He thought he saw a Garden Door
    That opened with a key:
He looked again, and found it was
    A Double-Rule-of-Three:
"And all its mystery," he said,
    "Is clear as day to me!"

CERVANTES

E. C. Bentley

The people of Spain think Cervantes
Equal to half-a-dozen Dantes:
An opinion resented most bitterly
By the people of Italy.

From *TRANSLATIONS FROM THE CHINESE*

Christopher Morley

HE COMFORTS HIMSELF

When I visited America
(It is the tedious Old Mandarin speaking)
I was eager to visit the birthplaces
Of Emily Dickinson and Louise Imogen Guiney,
And I found that this people
Had so neglected two of their greatest poets
That they hardly even knew their names.
But I was not peevish nor distraught:
I said to myself
Humanity is everywhere alike—
I myself am but little known in China.

A HUMAN INSTINCT

Youth is conservative,
Youth is the Tory,
Youth is the quencher of bright conflagration!

54

For whenever I light a match to kindle my pipe of opium
The young Mandarin and those quaint damsels his sisters
Competitively cry
O Sire, O Father, O Serene Progenitor,
May I blow it out?

SECRET THOUGHTS

And while my visitor prattled
I courteously nodded;
My eye was fast upon him,
My face bright with attention;
But inwardly I was saying:
"The excellent fellow, why does he tell me all this?
What has this to do with me?
O Buddha, when will he depart?"

THE MAN WITH THE RAKE

It is queer to think that many people
Have never raked leaves.
On a brilliant Sunday morning in October
I admired trees as ruddy as burnt orange,
Trees as pale and clear as Sauterne.
Raking placidly
I enjoyed the crisp rustle.

That is what I like about raking leaves—
It is wine and opiate for the mind:
The incessant skirmish of the wits is calmed,
And as you rake and burn

And dodge, with smarting eyes,
The pungent, veering reek,
You fall into a dull easy muse,
And think to yourself,
After all, what is writing books
But raking leaves?

And at such times
I plant the seeds of poems.
It takes poems a long while to grow—
They lie germinating in the dark of the mind;
But next spring, very likely,
There may emerge the green and tender shoots
Of two or three bright stanzas.

THE DARKLING THRUSH

Thomas Hardy

I leant upon a coppice gate
    When Frost was spectre-grey,
And Winter's dregs made desolate
    The weakening eye of day.
The tangled bine-stems scored the sky
    Like strings of broken lyres,
And all mankind that haunted night
    Had sought their household fires.

The land's sharp features seemed to be
    The Century's corpse outleant,
His crypt the cloudy canopy,
    The wind his death-lament.

56

The ancient pulse of germ and birth
      Was shrunken hard and dry,
And every spirit upon earth
      Seemed fervourless as I.

At once a voice arose among
      The bleak twigs overhead
In a full-hearted evensong
      Of joy illimited;
An aged thrush, frail, gaunt, and small,
      In blast-beruffled plume,
Had chosen thus to fling his soul
      Upon the growing gloom.

So little cause for carolings
      Of such ecstatic sound
Was written on terrestrial things
      Afar or nigh around,
That I could think there trembled through
      His happy good-night air
Some blessed Hope, whereof he knew
      And I was unaware.

                    December 1900

BARBER, BARBER . . .

Author Unknown

Barber, barber, shave a pig,
How many hairs will make a wig?
"Four-and-twenty, that's enough."
Give the barber a pinch of snuff.

Chorus from *ATALANTA IN CALYDON*

Algernon Charles Swinburne

When the hounds of spring are on winter's traces,
　　The mother of months in meadow or plain
Fills the shadows and windy places
　　With lisp of leaves and ripple of rain;

58

And the brown bright nightingale amorous
Is half assuaged for Itylus,
For the Thracian ships and the foreign faces,
     The tongueless vigil, and all the pain.

Come with bows bent and with emptying of quivers,
     Maiden most perfect, lady of light,
With a noise of winds and many rivers,
     With a clamour of waters, and with might;
Bind on thy sandals, O thou most fleet,
Over the splendour and speed of thy feet;
For the faint east quickens, the wan west shivers,
     Round the feet of the day and the feet of the night.

Where shall we find her, how shall we sing to her,
     Fold our hands round her knees, and cling?
O that man's heart were as fire and could spring to her,
     Fire, or the strength of the streams that spring!
For the stars and the winds are unto her
As raiment, as songs of the harp-player;
For the risen stars and the fallen cling to her,
     And the southwest-wind and the west-wind sing.

For winter's rains and ruins are over,
     And all the season of snows and sins;
The days dividing lover and lover,
     The light that loses, the night that wins;
And time remembered is grief forgotten,
And frosts are slain and flowers begotten,
And in green underwood and cover
     Blossom by blossom the spring begins.

The full streams feed on flower of rushes,
　　Ripe grasses trammel a travelling foot,
The faint fresh flame of the young year flushes
　　From leaf to flower and flower to fruit;
And fruit and leaf are as gold and fire,
And the oat is heard above the lyre,
And the hoofèd heel of a satyr crushes
　　The chestnut-husk at the chestnut-root.

And Pan by noon and Bacchus by night,
　　Fleeter of foot than the fleet-foot kid,
Follows with dancing and fills with delight
　　The Maenad and the Bassarid;
And soft as lips that laugh and hide
The laughing leaves of the trees divide,
And screen from seeing and leave in sight
　　The god pursuing, the maiden hid.

60

The ivy falls with the Bacchanal's hair
    Over her eyebrows hiding her eyes;
The wild vine slipping down leaves bare
    Her bright breast shortening into sighs;
The wild vine slips with the weight of its leaves,
But the berried ivy catches and cleaves
To the limbs that glitter, the feet that scare
    The wolf that follows, the fawn that flies.

FAREWELL TO THE FAIRIES

Richard Corbet

Farewell rewards and fairies,
    Good housewives now may say,
For now foul sluts in dairies
    Do fare as well as they.
And though they sweep their hearths no less
    Than maids were wont to do,
Yet who of late, for cleanliness,
    Finds sixpence in her shoe?

At morning and at evening both,
    You merry were and glad,
So little care of sleep or sloth
    Those pretty ladies had.
When Tom came home from labour,
    Or Cis to milking rose,
Then merrily went their tabor,
    And nimbly went their toes.

Witness those rings and roundelays
 Of theirs, which yet remain,
Were footed in Queen Mary's days
 On many a grassy plain;
But since of late Elizabeth,
 And later, James came in,
They never danced on any heath
 As when the time hath been.

By which we note the fairies
 Were of the old profession,
Their songs were Ave-Maries,
 Their dances were procession:
But now, alas! they all are dead,
 Or gone beyond the seas;
Or farther for religion fled,
 Or else they take their ease.

A tell-tale in their company
 They never could endure,
And whoso kept not secretly
 Their mirth, was punished sure;
It was a just and Christian deed
 To pinch such black and blue:
O how the commonwealth doth need
 Such justices as you!

A RUNNABLE STAG

John Davidson

When the pods went pop on the broom, green broom,
    And apples began to be golden-skinn'd,
We harbour'd a stag in the Priory coomb,
    And we feather'd his trail up-wind, up-wind,
    We feather'd his trail up-wind—
        A stag of warrant, a stag, a stag,
        A runnable stag, a kingly crop,
        Brow, bay and tray and three on top,
        A stag, a runnable stag.

Then the huntsman's horn rang yap, yap, yap,
    And 'Forwards' we heard the harbourer shout;
But 'twas only a brocket that broke a gap
    In the beeches underwood, driven out,
    From the underwood antler'd out
        By warrant and might of the stag, the stag,
        The runnable stag, whose lordly mind
        Was bent on sleep, though beam'd and tined
        He stood, a runnable stag.

So we tufted the covert till afternoon
    With Tinkerman's Pup and Bell-of-the-North;
And hunters were sulky and hounds out of tune
    Before we tufted the right stag forth,
    Before we tufted him forth,
        The stag of warrant, the wily stag,
        The runnable stag with his kingly crop,
        Brow, bay and tray and three on top,
        The royal and runnable stag.

It was Bell-of-the-North and Tinkerman's Pup
    That stuck to the scent till the copse was drawn.
'Tally ho! tally ho!' and the hunt was up,
    The tufters whipp'd and the pack laid on,
    The resolute pack laid on,
        And the stag of warrant away at last,
        The runnable stag, the same, the same,
        His hoofs on fire, his horns like flame,
        A stag, a runnable stag.

'Let your gelding be: if you check or chide
    He stumbles at once and you're out of the hunt;
For three hundred gentlemen, able to ride,
    On hunters accustom'd to bear the brunt,
    Accustom'd to bear the brunt,
        Are after the runnable stag, the stag,
        The runnable stag with his kingly crop,
        Brow, bay and tray and three on top,
        The right, the runnable stag.

By perilous paths in coomb and dell,
    The heather, the rocks, and the river-bed,
The pace grew hot, for the scent lay well,
    And a runnable stag goes right ahead,
    The quarry went right ahead—
        Ahead, ahead, and fast and far;
        His antler'd crest, his cloven hoof,
        Brow, bay and tray and three aloof,
        The stag, the runnable stag.

For a matter of twenty miles or more,
    By the densest hedge and the highest wall,

Through herds of bullocks he baffled the lore
  Of harbourer, huntsman, hounds and all,
  Of harbourer, hounds and all—
    The stag of warrant, the wily stag,
    For twenty miles, and five and five,
    He ran, and he never was caught alive,
    This stag, this runnable stag.

When he turn'd at bay in the leafy gloom
  In the emerald gloom where the brook ran deep
He heard in the distance the rollers boom,
  And he saw in a vision of peaceful sleep,
  A stag of warrant, a stag, a stag,
    A runnable stag in a jewell'd bed,
    Under the sheltering ocean dead,
    A stag, a runnable stag.

So a fateful hope lit up his eye,
  And he open'd his nostrils wide again,
And he toss'd his branching antlers high
  As he headed the hunt down the Charlock glen
  As he raced down the echoing glen—
    For five miles more, the stag, the stag,
    For twenty miles, and five and five,
    Not to be caught now, dead or alive,
    The stag, the runnable stag.

Three hundred gentlemen, able to ride,
  Three hundred horses as gallant and free,
Beheld him escape on the evening tide,
  Far out till he sank in the Severn Sea,
  Till he sank in the depths of the sea—

The stag, the buoyant stag, the stag
That slept at last in a jewell'd bed
Under the sheltering ocean spread,
The stag, the runnable stag.

MR. FLOOD'S PARTY

Edwin Arlington Robinson

Old Eben Flood, climbing alone one night
Over the hill between the town below
And the forsaken upland hermitage
That held as much as he should ever know
On earth again of home, paused warily.
The road was his with not a native near;
And Eben, having leisure, said aloud,
For no man else in Tilbury Town to hear:

'Well, Mr. Flood, we have the harvest moon
Again, and we may not have many more;
The bird is on the wing, the poet says,
And you and I have said it here before.
Drink to the bird.' He raised up to the light
The jug that he had gone so far to fill,
And answered huskily: 'Well, Mr. Flood,
Since you propose it, I believe I will.'

Alone, as if enduring to the end
A valiant armor of scarred hopes outworn,
He stood there in the middle of the road
Like Roland's ghost winding a silent horn.

66

Below him, in the town among the trees,
Where friends of other days had honored him,
A phantom salutation of the dead
Rang thinly till old Eben's eyes were dim.

Then, as a mother lays her sleeping child
Down tenderly, fearing it may awake,
He set the jug down slowly at his feet
With trembling care, knowing that most things break;
And only when assured that on firm earth
It stood, as the uncertain lives of men
Assuredly did not, he paced away,
And with his hand extended paused again:

'Well, Mr. Flood, we have not met like this
In a long time; and many a change has come
To both of us, I fear, since last it was
We had a drop together. Welcome home!'
Convivially returning with himself,
Again he raised the jug up to the light;
And with an acquiescent quaver said:
'Well, Mr. Flood, if you insist, I might.

'Only a very little, Mr. Flood—
For auld lang syne. No more, sir; that will do.'
So, for the time, apparently it did,
And Eben evidently thought so too;
For soon amid the silver loneliness
Of night he lifted up his voice and sang,
Secure, with only two moons listening,
Until the whole harmonious landscape rang—

'For auld lang syne.' The weary throat gave out,
The last word wavered, and the song was done.
He raised again the jug regretfully
And shook his head, and was again alone.
There was not much that was ahead of him,
And there was nothing in the town below—
Where strangers would have shut the many doors
That many friends had opened long ago.

OH, THE FUNNIEST THING . . .

Author Unknown

Oh, the funniest thing I've ever seen
Was a tomcat sewing on a sewing machine.
Oh, the sewing machine got running too slow,
And it took seven stitches in the tomcat's toe.

AN OLD SONG RE-SUNG

John Masefield

I saw a ship a-sailing, a-sailing, a-sailing,
With emeralds and rubies and sapphires in her hold;
And a bosun in a blue coat bawling at the railing,
Piping through a silver call that had a chain of gold;
The summer wind was falling and the tall ship rolled.

I saw a ship a-steering, a-steering, a-steering,
With roses in red thread worked upon her sails;
With sacks of purple amethysts, the spoils of buccaneering,
Skins of musky yellow wine, and silks in bales,
Her merry men were cheering, hauling in the brails.

I saw a ship a-sinking, a-sinking, a-sinking,
With glittering sea-water splashing on her decks,
With seamen in her spirit-room singing songs and drinking,
Pulling claret bottles down, and knocking off the necks,
The broken glass was chinking as she sank among the
       wrecks.

JENNY WREN

Author Unknown

Jenny Wren fell sick;
    Upon a merry time,
In came Robin Redbreast,
    And brought her sops of wine.

Eat well of the sop, Jenny,
    Drink well of the wine;
Thank you, Robin, kindly,
    You shall be mine.

Jenny she got well,
    And stood upon her feet,
And told Robin plainly
    She loved him not a bit.

Robin, being angry,
  Hopp'd on a twig,
Saying, Out upon you,
  Fie upon you,
    Bold-faced jig!

WHEN JACKY'S A VERY GOOD BOY

Mother Goose

When Jacky's a very good boy,
He shall have cakes and a custard;
But when he does nothing but cry,
He shall have nothing but mustard.

70

HOURS OF IDLENESS

George Gordon, Lord Byron

When Friendship or Love our sympathies move,
    When Truth in a glance should appear,
The lips may beguile with a dimple or smile,
    But the test of affection's a Tear. . . .

The man doom'd to sail with the blast of the gale,
    Through billows Atlantic to steer,
As he bends o'er the wave which may soon be his grave,
    The green sparkles bright with a Tear.

The soldier braves death for a fanciful wreath
    In Glory's romantic career;
But he raises the foe when in battle laid low,
    And bathes every wound with a Tear.

If with high-bounding pride he returns to his bride,
    Renouncing the gore-crimson'd spear,
All his toils are repaid when, embracing the maid,
    From her eyelid he kisses the Tear. . . .

Ye friends of my heart, ere from you I depart,
    This hope to my breast is most near:
If again we shall meet in this rural retreat,
    May we meet, as we part, with a Tear.

When my soul wings her flight to the regions of night,
    And my corpse shall recline on its bier,
As ye pass by the tomb where my ashes consume,
    Oh! moisten their dust with a Tear.

May no marble bestow the splendour of woe,
　　Which the children of vanity rear;
No fiction of fame shall blazon my name;
　　All I ask—all I wish—is a Tear.

THE OWL AND THE EEL AND THE WARMING-PAN

Laura E. Richards

The owl and the eel and the warming-pan,
They went to call on the soap-fat man.
The soap-fat man he was not within:
He'd gone for a ride on his rolling-pin.
So they all came back by the way of the town,
And turned the meeting-house upside down.

I EAT MY PEAS WITH HONEY . . .

Author Unknown

I eat my peas with honey;
I've done it all my life.
It makes the peas taste funny,
But it keeps them on the knife.

CROSS PATCH

Mother Goose

    Cross patch,
    Draw the latch,
Sit by the fire and spin;
    Take a cup,
    And drink it up,
Then call your neighbors in.

ANYONE LIVED IN A PRETTY HOW TOWN

e. e. cummings

anyone lived in a pretty how town
(with up so floating many bells down)
spring summer autumn winter
he sang his didn't he danced his did.

Women and men (both little and small)
cared for anyone not at all
they sowed their isn't they reaped their same
sun moon stars rain

children guessed (but only a few
and down they forgot as up they grew
autumn winter spring summer)
that noone loved him more by more

when by now and tree by leaf
she laughed his joy she cried his grief
bird by snow and stir by still
anyone's any was all to her

someones married their everyones
laughed their cryings and did their dance
(sleep wake hope and then) they
said their nevers they slept their dream

stars rain sun moon
(and only the snow can begin to explain
how children are apt to forget to remember
with up so floating many bells down)

one day anyone died i guess
(and noone stooped to kiss his face)
busy folk buried them side by side
little by little and was by was

all by all and deep by deep
and more by more they dream their sleep
noone and anyone earth by april
wish by spirit and if by yes.

Women and men (both dong and ding)
summer autumn winter spring
reaped their sowing and went their came
sun moon stars rain

WAY DOWN SOUTH . . .

Author Unknown

Way down South where bananas grow,
A grasshopper stepped on an elephant's toe.
The elephant said, with tears in his eyes,
"Pick on somebody your own size."

75

THE SHAKESPEAREAN BEAR

Arthur Guiterman

(*The Winter's Tale*, Act III, Scene 3)

When, on our casual way,
    Troubles and dangers accrue
Till there's the devil to pay,
    How shall we carry it through?
    Shakespeare, that oracle true,
Teacher in doubt and despair,
    Told us the best that he knew:
'Exit, pursued by a bear.'

That is the line of a play
    Dear to the cognizant few;
Hark to its lilt, and obey!
    Constantly keep it in view.
    Fate, the malevolent shrew,
Weaves her implacable snare;
    What is a fellow to do?
'Exit, pursued by a bear.'

Take to your heels while you may!
    Sinister tabby-cats mew,
Witches that scheme to betray
    Mingle their horrible brew,
    Thunderclouds darken the blue,
Beelzebub growls from his lair;
    Maybe he's hunting for *you!*—
'Exit, pursued by a bear.'

Bores of the dreariest hue,
    Bringers of worry and care,
Watch us respond to our cue,—
    'Exit, pursued by a bear.'

OLD QUIN QUEERIBUS

Nancy Byrd Turner

Old Quin Queeribus—
    He loved his garden so,
He wouldn't have a rake around,
    A shovel or a hoe.

For each potato's eyes he bought
    Fine spectacles of gold,
And mufflers for the corn, to keep
    Its ears from getting cold.

On every head of lettuce green—
    What do you think of that?
And every head of cabbage, too,
    He tied a garden hat.

Old Quin Queeribus—
    He loved his garden so,
He couldn't eat his growing things,
    He only let them grow!

RECUERDO

Edna St. Vincent Millay

We were very tired, we were very merry—
We had gone back and forth all night on the ferry.
It was bare and bright, and smelled like a stable—
But we looked into a fire, we leaned across a table,
We lay on a hill-top underneath the moon;
And the whistles kept blowing, and the dawn came soon.

We were very tired, we were very merry—
We had gone back and forth all night on the ferry;
And you ate an apple, and I ate a pear,
From a dozen of each we had bought somewhere;
And the sky went wan, and the wind came cold,
And the sun rose dripping, a bucketful of gold.

We were very tired, we were very merry,
We had gone back and forth all night on the ferry.
We hailed, "Good-morrow, mother!" to a shawl-covered
        head,
And bought a morning paper, which neither of us read;
And she wept, "God bless you!" for the apples and pears,
And we gave her all our money but our subway fares.

THE TAY BRIDGE DISASTER

William McGonagall

Beautiful Railway Bridge of the Silv'ry Tay!
Alas! I am very sorry to say
That ninety lives have been taken away

78

On the last Sabbath day of 1879,
Which will be remember'd for a very long time.

'Twas about seven o'clock at night,
And the wind it blew with all its might,
And the rain came pouring down,
And the dark clouds seem'd to frown,
And the Demon of the air seem'd to say—
"I'll blow down the Bridge of Tay."

When the train left Edinburgh
The passengers' hearts were light and felt no sorrow,
But Boreas blew a terrific gale,
Which made their hearts for to quail,
And many of the passengers with fear did say—
"I hope God will send us safe across the Bridge of Tay."

But when the train came near to Wormit Bay,
Boreas he did loud and angry bray,
And shook the central girders of the Bridge of Tay
On the last Sabbath day of 1879,
Which will be remember'd for a very long time.

So the train sped on with all its might,
And Bonnie Dundee soon hove in sight,
And the passengers' hearts felt light,
Thinking they would enjoy themselves on the New Year,
With their friends at home they lov'd most dear,
And wish them all a happy New Year.

So the train mov'd slowly along the Bridge of Tay,
Until it was about midway,

Then the central girders with a crash gave way,
And down went the train and passengers into the Tay!
The Storm Fiend did loudly bray,
Because ninety lives had been taken away,
On the last Sabbath day of 1879,
Which will be remember'd for a very long time.

As soon as the catastrophe came to be known
The alarm from mouth to mouth was blown,
And the cry rang out all o'er the town,
Good Heavens! the Tay Bridge is blown down,
And a passenger train from Edinburgh,
Which fill'd all the people's hearts with sorrow,
And made them for to turn pale,
Because none of the passengers were sav'd to tell the tale
How the disaster happen'd on the last Sabbath day of 1879,
Which will be remember'd for a very long time.

It must have been an awful sight,
To witness in the dusky moonlight,
While the Storm Fiend did laugh, and angry did bray,
Along the Railway Bridge of the Silv'ry Tay.
Oh! ill-fated Bridge of the Silv'ry Tay,
I must now conclude my lay
By telling the world fearlessly without the least dismay,
That your central girders would not have given way,
At least many sensible men do say,
Had they been supported on each side with buttresses,
At least many sensible men confesses,
For the stronger we our houses do build,
The less chance we have of being killed.

OLD MOTHER SHUTTLE

Author Unknown

Old Mother Shuttle
Lived in a coal-scuttle
Along with her dog and her cat;
What they ate I can't tell,
But 'tis known very well
That not one of the party was fat.

Old Mother Shuttle
Scoured out her coal-scuttle,
And washed both her dog and her cat;
The cat scratched her nose,
So they came to hard blows,
And who was the gainer by that?

ANTHEM FOR DOOMED YOUTH

Wilfred Owen

What passing-bells for these who die as cattle?
Only the monstrous anger of the guns.
Only the stuttering rifles' rapid rattle
Can patter out their hasty orisons.
No mockeries for them; no prayers nor bells,
Nor any voice of mourning save the choirs,—
The shrill, demented choirs of wailing shells;
And bugles calling for them from sad shires.
What candles may be held to speed them all?
Not in the hands of boys, but in their eyes

Shall shine the holy glimmers of good-byes.
The pallor of girls' brows shall be their pall;
Their flowers the tenderness of patient minds,
And each slow dusk a drawing-down of blinds.

THE OWL-CRITIC

J. T. Fields

'Who stuffed that white owl?' No one spoke in the shop.
The barber was busy, and he couldn't stop;
The customers, waiting their turns, were all reading
The 'Daily,' the 'Herald,' the 'Post,' little heeding
The young man who blurted out such a blunt question;
No one raised a head, or even made a suggestion;
        And the barber kept on shaving.

'Don't you see, Mr. Brown,'
Cried the youth, with a frown,
'How wrong the whole thing is,
How preposterous each wing is,
How flattened the head is, how jammed down the neck is—
In short, the whole owl, what an ignorant wreck 'tis!

I make no apology;
I've learned owl-eology.

'I've passed days and nights in a hundred collections,
And cannot be blinded to any deflections
Arising from unskillful fingers that fail
To stuff a bird right, from his beak to his tail.

Mister Brown! Mister Brown!
Do take that bird down,
Or you'll soon be the laughing-stock all over town!'
    And the barber kept on shaving.

'I've studied owls,
And other night fowls,
And I tell you
What I know to be true;
An owl cannot roost
With his limbs so unloosed:
No owl in the world
Ever had his claws curled,
Ever had his legs slanted,
Ever had his bill canted,
Ever had his neck screwed
Into that attitude.
He can't do it, because
'Tis against all bird-laws.

'Anatomy teaches,
Ornithology preaches,
An owl has a toe
That can't turn out so!
I've made the white owl my study for years,
And to see such a job almost moves me to tears!
Mr. Brown, I'm amazed
You should be so gone crazed
As to put up a bird
In that posture absurd!
To look at that owl really brings on a dizziness;
The man who stuffed him don't half know his business!'
    And the barber kept on shaving.

'Examine those eyes.
I'm filled with surprise
Taxidermists should pass
Off on you such poor glass;
So unnatural they seem
They'd make Audubon scream,
And John Burroughs laugh
To encounter such chaff.
Do take that bird down;
Have him stuffed again, Brown!'
    And the barber kept on shaving.

'With some sawdust and bark
I could stuff in the dark
An owl better than that.
I could make an old hat
Look more like an owl
Than that horrid fowl,
Stuck up there so stiff like a side of coarse leather.
In fact, about him there's not one natural feather.'

Just then, with a wink and a sly normal lurch,
The owl, very gravely, got down from his perch,
Walked round, and regarded his fault-finding critic
(Who thought he was stuffed) with a glance analytic,
And then fairly hooted, as if he should say:
'Your learning's at fault this time, anyway;
Don't waste it again on a live bird, I pray.
I'm an owl; you're another. Sir Critic, good day!'
    And the barber kept on shaving.

THE LION AND THE UNICORN

Author Unknown

The lion and the unicorn
    Were fighting for the crown;
The lion beat the unicorn
    All round the town.
Some gave them white bread,
    And some gave them brown;
Some gave them plum cake,
    And sent them out of town.

ELEGY IN A COUNTRY CHURCHYARD

G. K. Chesterton

The men that worked for England
They have their graves at home:
And bees and birds of England
About the cross can roam.

But they that fought for England,
Following a falling star,
Alas, alas for England
They have their graves afar.

And they that rule in England,
In stately conclave met,
Alas, alas for England
They have no graves as yet.

THE LITTLE GREEN ORCHARD

Walter de la Mare

Some one is always sitting there,
      In the little green orchard;
    Even when the sun is high
    In noon's unclouded sky,
    And faintly droning goes
    The bee from rose to rose,
Some one in shadow is sitting there,
      In the little green orchard.

86

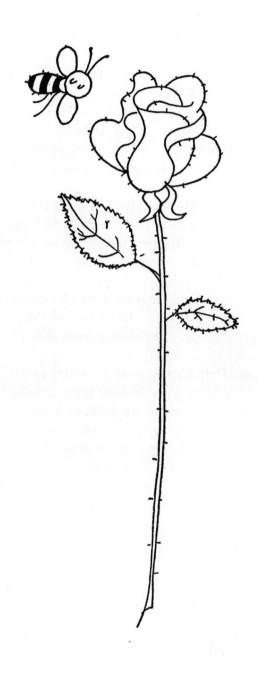

Yes, and when twilight is falling softly
        On the little green orchard;
    When the grey dew distils
    And every flower-cup fills;
    When the last blackbird says,
    'What—what!' and goes her way—S-sh!
I have heard voices calling softly
        In the little green orchard.

Not that I am afraid of being there,
        In the little green orchard;
    Why, when the moon's been bright,
    Shedding her lonesome light,
    And moths like ghosties come,
    And the horned snail leaves home:
I've sat there, whispering and listening there,
        In the little green orchard.

Only it's strange to be feeling there,
        In the little green orchard:
    Whether you paint or draw,
    Dig, hammer, chop, or saw;
    When you are most alone,
    All but the silence gone . . .
Some one is waiting and watching there,
        In the little green orchard.

BROWN'S DESCENT
or, THE WILLY-NILLY SLIDE

Robert Frost

Brown lived at such a lofty farm
    That everyone for miles could see
His lantern when he did his chores
    In winter after half-past three.

And many must have seen him make
    His wild descent from there one night,
'Cross lots, 'cross walls, 'cross everything,
    Describing rings of lantern light.

Between the house and barn the gale
    Got him by something he had on
And blew him out on the icy crust
    That cased the world, and he was gone!

Walls were all buried, trees were few:
    He saw no stay unless he stove
A hole in somewhere with his heel.
    But though repeatedly he strove

And stamped and said things to himself,
    And sometimes something seemed to yield,
He gained no foothold, but pursued
    His journey down from field to field.

Sometimes he came with arms outspread
    Like wings, revolving in the scene
Upon his longer axis, and
    With no small dignity of mien.

Faster or slower as he chanced,
        Sitting or standing as he chose,
According as he feared to risk
        His neck, or thought to spare his clothes,

He never let the lantern drop.
        And some exclaimed who saw afar
The figures he described with it,
        "I wonder what those signals are

"Brown makes at such an hour of night!
        He's celebrating something strange.
I wonder if he's sold his farm,
        Or been made Master of the Grange."

He reeled, he lurched, he bobbed, he checked;
        He fell and made the lantern rattle
(But saved the light from going out.)
        So halfway down he fought the battle,

Incredulous of his own bad luck.
        And then becoming reconciled
To everything, he gave it up
        And came down like a coasting child.

"Well—I—be—" that was all he said,
        As standing on the river road,
He looked back up the slippery slope
        (Two miles it was) to his abode.

Sometimes as an authority
        On motor-cars, I'm asked if I
Should say our stock was petered out,
        And this is my sincere reply:

90

Yankees are what they always were.
    Don't think Brown ever gave up hope
Of getting home again because
    He couldn't climb that slippery slope;

Or even thought of standing there
    Until the January thaw
Should take the polish off the crust.
    He bowed with grace to natural law,

And then went round it on his feet,
    After the manner of our stock;
Not much concerned for those to whom,
    At that particular time o'clock,

It must have looked as if the course
    He steered was straight away
From that which he was headed for—
    Not much concerned with them, I say;

No more so than became a man—
    And politician at odd seasons.
I've kept Brown waiting in the cold
    While I invested him with reasons;

But now he snapped his eyes three times;
    Then shook his lantern, saying "Ile's
'Bout out!" and took the long way home
    By road, a matter of several miles.

From *POEMS IN PRAISE OF PRACTICALLY
NOTHING*

Samuel Hoffenstein

You take a bath, and sit there bathing
In water cold, in water scathing;
You scrub till you're sans an epidermis
And feel like a regular bathing Hermes.
You do not waste a single minute;
The tub shows how you worked while in it;
You dry, and do some honest rooting
For such remarkable abluting.
Well, a day goes by, or ten, or thirty,
And what thanks do you get? You're just as dirty!

You hire a cook, but she can't cook yet;
You teach her by candle, bell, and book yet;
You show her, as if she were in her cradle,
To-day the soup, to-morrow a ladle.
Well, she doesn't learn, so although you need her
You decide that somebody else should feed her.
But you're kind by birth; you hate to fire her—
To tell a woman you don't require her.
So you wait and wait, and before you do it,
What thanks do you get? She beats you to it!

You leap out of bed; you start to get ready;
You dress and you dress till you feel unsteady;
Hours go by, and you're still busy
Putting on clothes, till your brain is dizzy.
Do you flinch, do you quit, do you go out naked?—
The least little button, you don't forsake it.
What thanks do you get? Well, for all this mess, yet
When night comes around you've got to undress yet.

THE CONCLUSION

Sir Walter Raleigh

Even such is Time, that takes in trust
    Our youth, our joys, our all we have,
And pays us but with earth and dust;
    Who in the dark and silent grave,
When we have wander'd all our ways,
Shuts up the story of our days;
But from this earth, this grave, this dust,
My God shall raise me up, I trust.

A CURSE ON THE CAT

John Skelton

O cat of churlish kind,
The fiend was in thy mind
When thou my bird untwin'd! [1]
The leopards savage,
The lions in their rage
Might catch thee in their paws,
And gnaw thee in their jaws!
The serpents of Libany
Might sting thee venomously!
The dragons with their tongues
Might poison thy liver and lungs!
The manticors [2] of the mountains
Might feed upon thy brains!

[1] untwin'd/destroyed   [2] manticors/human-headed dragons

THE DICK JOHNSON REEL

Jake Falstaff

(The old men say their grandfathers heard Dick Johnson sing the chorus of this song in the timberlands of northern Summit County, Ohio.)

Old Dick Johnson, gentleman, adventurer,
Braggart, minstrel, lover of a brawl,
Walked in the timber from Northfield to Hudson.
(Backward, forward and sashay all!)

Old Dick Johnson, joker and wanderer,
Poet, vagabond and beater of the track,
Sang a song of his bravery and prowess:
(Ladies go forward and gents go back!)

Chorus:

Ripsi, rantsi,
Humpsy, dumpsy;
I, Dick Johnson,
Killed Tecumseh!

Old Dick Johnson, fighter of the Indians,
Sang from Boston to the hills of Bath;
Sang the song of his muscle and his musket.
(Swing your partners and leave a path!)
The redskin sleeps where the wheat is growing,
But old Dick Johnson's ghost is free,
And it sings all night from Richfield to Twinsburg:
(All hands 'round with a one-two-three!)

Chorus:

Ripsi, rantsi,
Humpsy, dumpsy;
I, Dick Johnson,
Killed Tecumseh!

THE PILGRIM

John Bunyan

Who would true valour see,
Let him come hither;
One here will constant be,
Come wind, come weather.
There's no discouragement
Shall make him once relent
His first avowed intent
To be a Pilgrim.

Who so beset him round
With dismal stories
Do but themselves confound;
His strength the more is.
No lion can him fright,
But he will have a right
To be a Pilgrim.

Hobgoblin nor foul fiend
Can daunt his spirit:
He knows he at the end
Shall life inherit.
Then fancies fly away,
He'll fear not what men say,
He'll labour night and day
To be a Pilgrim.

TOM O' BEDLAM'S SONG

Author Unknown

From the hag and hungry goblin
That into rags would rend ye
And the spirit that stands by the naked man
In the Book of Moons defend ye!
That of your five sound senses
You never be forsaken
Nor wander from your selves with Tom
Abroad to beg your bacon.
    While I do sing 'Any food, any feeding,
    Feeding, drink or clothing.'
    Come dame or maid, be not afraid,
    Poor Tom will injure nothing. . . .

With a thought I took for Maudlin
And a cruse of cockle pottage,
With a thing thus tall, sky bless you all,
I befell into this dotage.
I slept not since the Conquest,
Till then I never wakèd
Till the roguish boy of love where I lay
Me found and stripped me naked.
    And now I sing 'Any food, any feeding,
    Feeding, drink or clothing,'
    Come dame or maid, be not afraid,
    Poor Tom will injure nothing. . . .

When I short have shorn my sour face
And swigged my horny barrel

In an oaken inn I pound my skin
As a suit of gilt apparel.
The moon's my constant Mistress
And the lowly owl my marrow;
The flaming Drake and the Nightcrow make
Me music to my sorrow.
> While I do sing 'Any food, any feeding,
> Feeding, drink or clothing.'
> Come dame or maid, be not afraid,
> Poor Tom will injure nothing. . . .

I know more than Apollo,
For oft when he lies sleeping
I see the stars at bloody wars
In the wounded welkin weeping,
The moon embrace her shepherd
And the queen of Love her warrior,
While the first doth horn the star of morn
And the next the heavenly Farrier,
> While I do sing 'Any food, any feeding,
> Feeding, drink or clothing.'
> Come dame or maid, be not afraid,
> Poor Tom will injure nothing. . . .

With a host of furious fancies
Whereof I am commander,
With a burning spear, and a horse of air,
To the wilderness I wander.
By a knight of ghosts and shadows
I summoned am to tourney
Ten leagues beyond the wide world's end.
Methinks it is no journey.

Yet will I sing 'Any food, any feeding,
Feeding, drink or clothing.'
Come dame or maid, be not afraid,
Poor Tom will injure nothing.

THE DEATH OF PRINCE LEOPOLD

William McGonagall

Alas! noble Prince Leopold, he is dead!
Who often has his lustre shed:
Especially by singing for the benefit of Esher School,—
Which proves he was a wise prince, and no conceited fool.

Methinks I see him on the platform singing the *Sands o'
    Dee*,
The generous-hearted Leopold, the good and the free,
Who was manly in his actions, and beloved by his mother;
And in all the family she hasn't got such another.

He was of a delicate constitution all his life,
And he was his mother's favourite, and very kind to his
        wife,
And he had also a particular liking for his child,
And in his behaviour he was very mild.

Oh! noble-hearted Leopold, most beautiful to see,
Who was wont to fill your audience's heart with glee,
With your charming songs, and lectures against strong
        drink:
Britain had nothing else to fear, as far as you could
        think. . . .

THERE WAS AN OLD WOMAN . . .

Author Unknown

There was an old woman tossed up in a basket
Seventeen times as high as the Moon;
Where she was going I couldn't but ask it,
For in her hand she carried a broom.
'Old woman, old woman, old woman,' quoth I,
'Where are you going to, up so high?'
'To sweep the cobwebs from the sky!'
'May I go with you?' 'Yes, by-and-by.'

WE HAVE BEEN HERE BEFORE

Morris Bishop

I think I remember this moorland,
 The tower on the tip of the tor;
I feel in the distance another existence;
 I think I have been here before.

And I think you were sitting beside me
 In a fold in the face of the fell;
For Time at its work'll go round in a circle,
 And what is befalling, befell.

'I have been here before!' I asserted,
 In a nook on the neck of the Nile.
I once in a crisis was punished by Isis,
 And you smiled, I remember your smile.

100

I had the same sense of persistence
   On the site of the seat of the Sioux;
I heard in the tepee the sound of a sleepy
   Pleistocene grunt. It was you.

The past made a promise, before it
   Began to begin to begone.
This limited gamut brings you again. . . . Damn it,
   How long has this got to go on?

SWANS SING . . .

S. T. Coleridge

Swans sing before they die—'twere no bad thing
Should certain persons die before they sing.

YANKEE CRADLE

Robert P. Tristram Coffin

So lucky I was in being born
Under Huckleberry Hump on Cranberryhorn!
Learned to cry from the whippoorwill
In the ocean fogs on Misery Hill!

My first brief steps I took between
Buttermilk Bridge and Bombazeen,
I learned to coast down belly-butt
On the balsam shores of Prince's Gut.

I learned to tread a load of hay
On a sea-going farm on Quahaug Bay,
Squirrels for me meant Robin Hood,
New Meadows Church was God and good.

A boy is lucky to play his games
Among such stout American names,
Drink buttermilk from an earthen noggin
By Mount Ararat on the Androscoggin.

The *Bible* and Indians named my places
With names like bronze and lobstermen's faces—
Shiloh, Merryconeag, Cathance,
Sabbath Day Lake, and Winnegance.

Yankee as the heron's speech,
Whizzgig Creek and Fiddler's Reach,
My places marked me with the burrs,
With tasselled maize and steepled firs.

Merrymeeting, Bold Dick, the Ram
Made me the Yankee that I am,
Wild geese cried the night I was born,
And the fog rolled high on Cranberryhorn.

LIMERICKS

Edward Lear

There was an Old Man of The Hague,
Whose ideas were excessively vague;
    He built a balloon
    To examine the moon,
That deluded Old Man of The Hague.

There was an Old Man of Thermopylae,
Who never did anything properly;
    But they said: 'If you choose
    To boil Eggs in your Shoes,
You shall never remain in Thermopylae!'

There was an Old Person of Ickley,
Who could not abide to ride quickly;
    He rode to Karnak
    On a Tortoise's back,
That moony Old Person of Ickley.

There was an Old Man who said: 'How
Shall I flee from that horrible cow?
    I will sit on this stile,
    And continue to smile,
Which may soften the heart of that cow.'

THE HEN AND THE ORIOLE

Don Marquis

well boss did it
ever strike you that a
hen regrets it just as
much when they wring her
neck as an oriole but
nobody has any
sympathy for a hen because
she is not beautiful
while every one gets
sentimental over the
oriole and says how
shocking to kill the
lovely thing this thought
comes to my mind
because of the earnest
endeavor of a
gentleman to squash me
yesterday afternoon when i
was riding up in the
elevator if i had been a
butterfly he would have
said how did that
beautiful thing happen to
find its way into
these grimy city streets do
not harm the splendid
creature but let it
fly back to its rural
haunts again beauty always

104

gets the best of
it be beautiful boss
a thing of beauty is a
joy forever
be handsome boss and let
who will be clever is
the sad advice
of your ugly little friend
                              archy

EVE

Ralph Hodgson

Eve, with her basket, was
Deep in the bells and grass,
Wading in bells and grass
Up to her knees,
Picking a dish of sweet
Berries and plums to eat,
Down in the bells and grass
Under the trees.

Mute as a mouse in a
Corner the cobra lay,
Curled round a bough of the
Cinnamon tall. . . .
Now to get even and
Humble proud heaven and—
Now was the moment or
Never at all.

'Eva!' each syllable
Light as a flower fell,
'Eva!' he whispered the
Wondering maid,
Soft as a bubble sung
Out of a linnet's lung,
Soft and most silverly
'Eva!' he said.

Picture that orchard sprite,
Eve, with her body white,
Supple and smooth to her
Slim finger tips,
Wondering, listening,
Listening, wondering,
Eve with a berry
Half-way to her lips.

Oh, had our simple Eve
Seen through the make-believe!
Had she but known the
Pretender he was!
Out of the boughs he came,
Whispering still her name,
Tumbling in twenty rings
Into the grass.

Here was the strangest pair
In the world anywhere
Even in the bells and grass
Kneeling, and he
Telling his story low. . . .
Singing birds saw them go

Down the dark path to
The Blasphemous Tree.

Oh, what a clatter when
Titmouse and Jenny Wren
Saw him successful and
Taking his leave!
How the birds rated him!
How they all hated him!
How they all pitied
Poor motherless Eve!

Picture her crying,
Outside in the lane,
Eve, with no dish of sweet
Berries and plums to eat,
Haunting the gate of the
Orchard in vain. . . .
Picture that lewd delight
Under the hill to-night—
'Eva!' the toast goes round,
'Eva!' again.

A LYKE-WAKE DIRGE

Author Unknown

This ae nighte, this ae nighte,
    —*Every nighte and alle,*
Fire and fleet and candle-lighte,
    And Christe receive thy saule.

When thou from hence away art past,
   —*Every nighte and alle,*
To Whinny-muir thou com'st at last;
   And Christe receive thy saule.

If ever thou gavest hosen and shoon,
   —*Every nighte and alle,*
Sit thee down and put them on;
   And Christe receive thy saule.

If hosen and shoon thou ne'er gav'st nane,
   —*Every nighte and alle,*
The whinnies sall prick thee to the bare bane;
   And Christe receive thy saule.

From Whinny-muir when thou may'st pass,
   —*Every nighte and alle,*
To Brig o' Dread thou com'st at last;
   And Christe receive thy saule.

From Brig o' dread when thou may'st pass,
   —*Every nighte and alle,*
To Purgatory fire thou com'st at last;
   And Christe receive thy saule.

If ever thou gavest meat or drink,
   —*Every nighte and alle,*
The fire sall never make thee shrink,
   And Christe receive thy saule.

If meat or drink thou ne'er gav'st nane,
   —*Every nighte and alle,*

108

The fire will burn thee to the bare bane;
And Christe receive thy saule.

This ae nighte, this ae nighte,
　　—Every nighte and alle,
Fire and fleet and candle-lighte,
　　And Christe receive thy saule.

AND SHALL TRELAWNY DIE?

R. S. Hawker

A good sword and a trusty hand!
　　A merry heart and true!
King James's men shall understand
　　What Cornish lads can do.

And have they fixed the where and when?
　　And shall Trelawny die?
Here's twenty thousand Cornish men
　　Will know the reason why!

Out spake their captain brave and bold,
　　A merry wight was he:
'If London Tower were Michael's hold,
　　We'll set Trelawny free!

'We'll cross the Tamar, land to land,
　　The Severn is no stay,
With "one and all," and hand in hand,
　　And who shall bid us nay?

'And when we come to London Wall,
    A pleasant sight to view,
Come forth! come forth, ye cowards all,
    Here's men as good as you.

'Trelawny he's in keep and hold,
    Trelawny he may die;
But here's twenty thousand Cornish bold
    Will know the reason why!'

THE WAR SONG OF DINAS VAWR

Thomas Love Peacock

The mountain sheep are sweeter,
But the valley sheep are fatter;
We therefore deemed it meeter
To carry off the latter.
We made an expedition;
We met a host and quelled it;
We forced a strong position,
And killed the men who held it.

On Dyfed's richest valley,
Where herds of kine were browsing,
We made a mighty sally,
To furnish our carousing.
Fierce warriors rushed to meet us;
We met them, and o'er threw them:
They struggled hard to beat us;
But we conquered them, and slew them.

110

As we drove our prize at leisure,
The king marched forth to catch us:
His rage surpassed all measure,
But his people could not match us.
He fled to his hall-pillars;
And, ere our force we led off,
Some sacked his house and cellars
While others cut his head off.

We there, in strife bewildering,
Spilt blood enough to swim in:
We orphaned many children,
And widowed many women.
The eagles and the ravens
We glutted with our foemen;
The heroes and the cravens,
The spearmen and the bowmen.

We brought away from battle,
And much their land bemoaned them,
Two thousand head of cattle,
And the head of him who owned them:
Ednyfed, King of Dyfed,
His head was borne before us;
His wine and beasts supplied our feasts,
And his overthrow, our chorus.

THE HUNTER

Ogden Nash

The hunter crouches in his blind
'Neath camouflage of every kind,
And conjures up a quacking noise
To lend allure to his decoys.
This grown-up man, with pluck and luck,
Is hoping to outwit a duck.

WHY SO PALE AND WAN?

Sir John Suckling

Why so pale and wan, fond lover?
    Prithee, why so pale?
Will, when looking well can't move her,
    Looking ill prevail?
    Prithee, why so pale?

Why so dull and mute, young sinner?
    Prithee, why so mute?
Will, when speaking well can't win her,
    Saying nothing do 't?
    Prithee, why so mute?

Quit, quit for shame! This will not move;
    This cannot take her.
If of herself she will not love,
    Nothing can make her:
    The devil take her!

112

THE LLAMA

Hilaire Belloc

The Llama is a woolly sort of fleecy hairy goat,
With an indolent expression and an undulating throat
    Like an unsuccessful literary man.
And I know the place he lives in (or at least—I think I do)
It is Ecuador, Brazil or Chile—possibly Peru;
    You must find it in the Atlas if you can.
The Llama of the Pampasses you never should confound
(In spite of a deceptive similarity of sound)
    With the Lhama who is Lord of Turkestan.

113

For the former is a beautiful and valuable beast,
But the latter is not lovable nor useful in the least;
And the Ruminant is preferable surely to the Priest
Who battens on the woful superstitions of the East,
    The Mongol of the Monastery of Shan.

THE OLD SHIPS

James Elroy Flecker

I have seen old ships sail like swans asleep
Beyond the village which men still call Tyre,
With leaden age o'ercargoed, dipping deep
For Famagusta and the hidden sun
That rings black Cyprus with a lake of fire;
And all those ships were certainly so old—
Who knows how oft with squat and noisy gun,
Questing brown slaves or Syrian oranges,
The pirate Genoese
Hell-raked them till they rolled
Blood, water, fruit and corpses up the hold.
But now through friendly seas they softly run,
Painted the mid-sea blue or shore-sea green,
Still patterned with the vine and grapes in gold.

But I have seen
Pointing her shapely shadows from the dawn
And image tumbled on a rose-swept bay,
A drowsy ship of some yet older day;

And, wonder's breath indrawn,
Thought I—who knows—who knows—but in that same
(Fished up beyond Aeaea, patched up new
—Stern painted brighter blue—)
That talkative, bald-headed seaman came
(Twelve patient comrades sweating at the oar)
From Troy's doom-crimson shore,
And with great lies about his wooden horse
Set the crew laughing, and forgot his course.

It was so old a ship—who knows, who knows?
—And yet so beautiful, I watched in vain
To see the mast burst open with a rose,
And the whole deck put on its leaves again.

SPRING AND ALL

William Carlos Williams

so much depends
upon

a red wheel
barrow

glazed with rain
water

beside the white
chickens

I TOOK A BOW AND ARROW

John Ciardi

I took a bow and arrow
(I don't know where I got it.
I may have found it somewhere.
Perhaps I even bought it.)

However it was, I took it
And shot it straight and true
At a Polar Bear in Washington Square
And hit a policeman's shoe.

Some say it was the left shoe.
Some say it was the right.
Some say it wasn't a Polar Bear
But a Cinnamon Yak dyed white.

It really doesn't matter,
But I *know* it was a Bear:
Whoever saw a Cinnamon Yak
In the middle of Washington Square!

FE, FI, FO, FUM . . .

Author Unknown

Fe, fi, fo, fum,
I smell the blood of an Englishman!
Be he alive or be he dead,
I'll grind his bones to make my bread!

116

TO CHRISTOPHER NORTH

Alfred, Lord Tennyson

You did late review my lays,
    Crusty Christopher;
You did mingle blame and praise,
    Rusty Christopher.

When I learned from whom it came,
I forgave you all the blame,
    Musty Christopher;
I could *not* forgive the praise,
    Fusty Christopher.

POTOMAC TOWN IN FEBRUARY

Carl Sandburg

The bridge says: Come across, try me; see how
    good I am.
The big rock in the river says: Look at me;
    learn how to stand up.
The white water says: I go on; around, under,
    over, I go on.
A kneeling, scraggly pine says: I am here yet;
    they nearly got me last year.
A sliver of moon slides by on a high wind calling:
    I know why; I'll see you tomorrow; I'll tell
    you everything tomorrow.

117

OUR SILLY LITTLE SISTER
Dorothy Aldis

To begin with she wouldn't have fallen in
If she hadn't been acting so silly.
First thing we saw was her hair ribbon there
On top like a water lily.

In less than a minute we'd gotten her out
And set her down quickly to drain,
And do you know what she said through her
       dripping hair?
"I want to go swimming again."

"Swimming?" we cried. "Do you think
      you can swim?"
She sat there so scowly and black.
"Much better than you can, besides I
      don't care!"
We couldn't think what to say back.

NUTS AN' MAY

Author Unknown

Here we come gathering nuts an' may,
    Nuts an' may, nuts an' may;
Here we come gathering nuts an' may,
    On a fine and frosty morning.

Pray who will you gather for nuts an' may,
    Nuts an' may, nuts an' may;
Pray who will you gather for nuts an' may,
    On a fine and frosty morning?

We'll gather Mary for nuts an' may,
    Nuts an' may, nuts an' may;
We'll gather Mary for nuts an' may,
    On a fine and frosty morning.

Who'll you send to take her away,
    Take her away, take her away;
Pray who'll you send to take her away,
    On a fine and frosty morning?

We'll send Johnny Smith to take her away,
    Take her away, take her away;
We'll send Johnny Smith to take her away,
    On a fine and frosty morning.

THE LOOKING-GLASS
(A Country Dance)

Rudyard Kipling

Queen Bess was Harry's daughter. Stand forward
        partners all!
In ruff and stomacher and gown
She danced King Philip down-a-down,
And left her shoe to show 'twas true—
        (The very tune I'm playing you)
In Norgem at Brickwall!

The Queen was in her chamber, and she was middling old.
Her petticoat was satin, and her stomacher was gold.
Backwards and forwards and sideways did she pass,
Making up her mind to face the cruel looking-glass.
The cruel looking-glass that will never show a lass
As comely or as kindly as what she was!
Queen Bess was Harry's daughter. Now hand your partners
        all!

The Queen was in her chamber, a-combing of her hair.
There came Queen Mary's spirit and It stood behind her
        chair,
Singing 'Backwards and forwards and sideways may you
        pass,
But I will stand behind you till you face the looking-glass.
The cruel looking-glass that will never show a lass
As lovely or unlucky or as lonely as I was!'
Queen Bess was Harry's daughter. Now turn your partners
        all!

The Queen was in her chamber, a-weeping very sore,
There came Lord Leicester's spirit and It scratched upon
        the door,
Singing 'Backwards and forwards and sideways may you
        pass,
But I will walk beside you till you face the looking-glass.
The cruel looking-glass that will never show a lass,
As hard and unforgiving or as wicked as you was!'
Queen Bess was Harry's daughter. Now kiss your partners
        all!

The Queen was in her chamber, her sins were on her head.
She looked the spirits up and down and statelily she said:—
'Backwards and forwards and sideways though I've been,
Yet I am Harry's daughter and I am England's Queen!'
And she faced the looking-glass (and whatever else there
        was)
And she saw her day was over and she saw her beauty pass
In the cruel looking-glass, that can always hurt a lass
More hard than any ghost there is or any man there was!

THE ASHTABULA DISASTER

Julia Moore

Have you heard of the dreadful fate
    Of Mr. P. P. Bliss and wife?
Of their death I will relate,
    And also others lost their life;
Ashtabula Bridge disaster,
Where so many people died
Without a thought that destruction
    Would plunge them 'neath the wheel of tide.

Chorus

    Swiftly passed the engine's call,
        Hastening souls on to death,
    Warning not one of them all;
        It brought despair right and left.

Among the ruins are many friends,
    Crushed to death amidst the roar,
On one thread all may depend,
    And hope they've reached the other shore.
P. P. Bliss showed great devotion
    To his faithful wife, his pride,
When he saw that she must perish
    He died a martyr by her side.

P. P. Bliss went home above—
    Left all friends, earth, and fame,
To rest in God's holy love;
    Left on earth his work and name.

122

The people love his work by numbers,
　　It is read by great and small,
He by it will be remembered,
　　He has left it for us all.

His good name from time to time
　　Will rise on land and sea;
It is known in distant climes,
　　Let it echo wide and free.
One good man among the number,
　　Found sweet rest in a short time,
His weary soul may sweetly slumber
　　Within the vale, heaven sublime.

A FARMER WENT TROTTING . . .

Author Unknown

A farmer went trotting upon his grey mare,
　　Bumpety, bumpety, bump!
With his daughter behind him so rosy and fair,
　　Lumpety, lumpety, lump!

A raven cried croak! and they all tumbled down,
　　Bumpety, bumpety, bump!
The mare broke her knees, and the farmer his crown,
　　Lumpety, lumpety, lump!

The mischievous raven flew laughing away,
　　Bumpety, bumpety, bump!
And vowed he would serve them the same the next day,
　　Lumpety, lumpety, lump!

THE HUMORIST

Keith Preston

He must not laugh at his own wheeze:
A snuff box has no right to sneeze.

From *THE STORY OF RIMINI*

Leigh Hunt

Ready she sat with one hand to turn o'er
The leaf, to which her thoughts ran on before,
The other on the table, half enwreath'd
In the thick tresses over which she breath'd.
So sat she fix'd, and so observ'd was she
Of one, who at the door stood tenderly,—
Paolo,—who from a window seeing her
Go straight across the lawn, and guessing where,
Had thought she was in tears, and found, that day,
His usual efforts vain to keep away.
Twice had he seen her since the Prince was gone,
On some small matter needing unison;
Twice linger'd, and convers'd, and grown long friends;
But not till now where no one else attends.—
"May I come in?" said he:—it made her start,—
That smiling voice;—she colour'd, press'd her heart
A moment, as for breath, and then with free
And usual tone said,—"O yes, certainly."

THE YARN OF THE *NANCY BELL*

W. S. Gilbert

'Twas on the shores that round our coast
　　From Deal to Ramsgate span,
That I found alone on a piece of stone
　　An elderly naval man.

His hair was weedy, his beard was long,
　　And weedy and long was he,
And I heard this wight on the shore recite,
　　In a singular minor key:

"Oh, I am a cook and a captain bold,
　　And the mate of the *Nancy* brig,
And a bo'sun tight, and a midshipmite,
　　And the crew of the captain's gig."

And he shook his fists and he tore his hair,
　　Till I really felt afraid,
For I couldn't help thinking the man had been drinking,
　　And so I simply said:

"Oh, elderly man, it's little I know
　　Of the duties of men of the sea,
But I'll eat my hat if I understand
　　How you can possibly be

"At once a cook, and a captain bold,
　　And the mate of the *Nancy* brig,
And a bo'sun tight and a midshipmite,
　　And the crew of the captain's gig."

Then he gave a hitch to his trousers, which
    Is a trick all seamen larn,
And having got rid of a thumping quid,
    He spun this painful yarn:

" 'Twas in the good ship *Nancy Bell*
    That we sailed to the Indian sea,
And there on a reef we come to grief,
    Which has often occurred to me.

"And pretty nigh all o' the crew was drowned
    (There were seventy-seven o' soul),
And only ten of the *Nancy's* men
    Said 'Here!' to the muster-roll.

"There was me and the cook and the captain bold,
    And the mate of the *Nancy* brig,
And the bo'sun tight and the midshipmite,
    And the crew of the captain's gig.

"For a month we'd neither wittles nor drink,
    Till a-hungry we did feel,
So we drawed a lot, and accordin' shot
    The captain for our meal.

"The next lot fell to the *Nancy's* mate,
    And a delicate dish he made;
Then our appetite with the midshipmite
    We seven survivors stayed.

"And then we murdered the bo'sun tight,
    And he much resembled pig;

126

Then we wittled free, did the cook and me,
    On the crew of the captain's gig.

"Then only the cook and me was left,
    And the delicate question, 'Which
Of us two goes to the kettle?' arose
    And we argued it out as sich.

"For I loved that cook as a brother, I did,
    And the cook he worshipped me;
But we'd both be blowed if we'd either be stowed
    In the other chap's hold, you see.

" 'I'll be eat if you dines off me,' says TOM,
    'Yes, that,' says I, 'you'll be,'—
'I'm boiled if I died, my friend,' quoth I,
    And 'Exactly so,' quoth he.

"Says he, 'Dear JAMES, to murder me
    Were a foolish thing to do,
For don't you see that you can't cook *me*,
    While I can—and will—cook *you!*'

"So he boils the water, and takes the salt
    And the pepper in portions true
(Which he never forgot), and some chopped shallot,
    And some sage and parsley too.

" 'Come here,' says he, with a proper pride,
    Which his smiling features tell,
' 'Twill soothing be if I let you see,
    How extremely nice you'll smell.'

"And he stirred it round and round and round,
    And he sniffed at the foaming froth;
When I ups with his heels, and smothers his squeals
    In the scum of the boiling broth.

"And I eat that cook in a week or less,
    And—as I eating be
The last of his chops, why, I almost drops,
    For a wessel in sight I see!

      *   *   *   *   *   *   *   *

"And I never grin, and I never smile,
    And I never larf nor play,
But I sit and croak, and a single joke
    I have—which is to say:

"Oh, I am a cook and a captain bold,
    And the mate of the *Nancy* brig,
And a bosun tight, *and* a midshipmite,
    And the crew of the captain's gig!"

COLLY, MY COW

Author Unknown

Little Tom Dogget,
    What dost thou mean,
To kill thy poor Colly,
    Now she's so lean?
        Sing, oh poor Colly,
            Colly, my cow;
        For Colly will give me
            No more milk now.

Oh, if I have killed her
I can't her recall;
I will sell my poor Colly,
Hide, horns, and all.
Sing, oh poor Colly.

Now, in comes the tanner,
His sword by his side,
He bids me five shillings
For my poor cow's hide.
Sing, oh poor Colly.

And in comes the huntsman
So early at morn,
He bids me a penny
For my poor cow's horn.
Sing, oh poor Colly.

Poor Colly each year
A fine calf did me bring,
Which fetched me a pound,
For it came in the spring.
Sing, oh poor Colly.

The skin of my cowly
Was softer than silk,
And three times a day
My poor cow would give milk.
*Sing, oh poor Colly,
Colly, my cow;
For Colly will give me
No more milk now!*

PRESENTS

Marchette Chute

I wanted a rifle for Christmas
    I wanted a bat and a ball,
I wanted some skates and a bicycle,
    But I didn't want mittens at all.

        I wanted a whistle
            And I wanted a kite,
        I wanted a pocketknife
            That shut up tight.
        I wanted some books
            And I wanted a kit,
But I didn't want mittens one little bit.

I told them I didn't like mittens,
    I told them as plain as plain.
I told them I didn't WANT mittens
    And they've given me mittens again!

THE BIRD'S NEST

John Drinkwater

I know a place, in the ivy on a tree,
Where a bird's nest is, and the eggs are three,
And the bird is brown, and the eggs are blue,
And the twigs are old, but the moss is new,
And I go quite near, though I think I should have heard
The sound of me watching, if I had been a bird.

130

ONE BRIGHT MORNING . . .

Author Unknown

One bright morning in the middle of the night
Two dead boys got up to fight.
Back to back they faced each other,
Drew their swords and shot each other.
A deaf policeman heard the noise
And came and killed those two dead boys.

THE PRODIGY

A. P. Herbert

I kissed my darling at the Zoo,
    And all the people snorted,
The keeper took his little book
    And said we'd be reported;
But the Small Birds sang, though a trifle flat,
And the Pelican said, "Now, fancy that!"
    In a sentimental fashion,
The Elephant sighed and went quite pale,
And the Dromedary told a tedious tale
    Of a grand but youthful passion.

> *The Lion no more did roar,*
>   *And I heard the Eagles coo.*
> *For I never had kissed my Jane before,*
>   *And I kissed her at the Zoo.*

I kissed my darling at the Zoo—
    The people left off gazing
At camel and cod and kangaroo,
    For we were more amazing;
The Octopus and the Chimpanzee
Were shocked when they looked out to see
    The usual crowd was missing,
While swarming round us, goggle-eyed,
"Ma, look at that!" the children cried,
    "Two funny creatures kissing!"

        But the Lion no more did roar,
        And I heard the Eagles coo.
        For I never had kissed my Jane before,
        And I kissed her at the Zoo.

LOCHINVAR

Sir Walter Scott

O, young Lochinvar is come out of the west,
Through all the wide Border his steed was the best;
And, save his good broadsword, he weapon had none,
He rode all unarmed, and he rode all alone.
So faithful in love, and so dauntless in war,
There never was knight like the young Lochinvar.

He stayed not for brake, and he stopped not for stone,
He swam the Eske River where ford there was none;

But ere he alighted at Netherby gate,
The bride had consented, the gallant came late;
For a laggard in love, and a dastard in war,
Was to wed the fair Ellen of brave Lochinvar.

So boldly he entered the Netherby Hall,
Among bridesmen, and kinsmen, and brothers, and all.
Then spoke the bride's father, his hand on his sword
(For the poor craven bridegroom said never a word),
"O, come ye in peace here, or come ye in war,
Or to dance at our bridal, young Lord Lochinvar?"

"I long wooed your daughter, my suit you denied;—
Love swells like the Solway, but ebbs like its tide,—
And now I am come, with this lost love of mine,
To lead but one measure, drink one cup of wine.
There are maidens in Scotland more lovely by far,
That would gladly be bride to the young Lochinvar."

The bride kissed the goblet; the knight took it up,
He quaffed off the wine, and he threw down the cup.
She looked down to blush, and she looked up to sigh,
With a smile on her lips, and a tear in her eye.
He took her soft hand, ere her mother could bar,—
"Now tread we a measure!" said young Lochinvar.

So stately his form, and so lovely her face,
That never a hall such a galliard did grace;
While her mother did fret, and her father did fume,
And the bridegroom stood dangling his bonnet and plume;
And the bridemaidens whispered, " 'Twere better by far,
To have matched our fair cousin with young Lochinvar."

134

One touch to her hand, and one word in her ear,
When they reached the hall-door, and the charger stood
      near.
So light to the croupe the fair lady he swung,
So light to the saddle before her he sprung!
"She is won! we are gone! over bank, bush, and scaur;
They'll have fleet steeds that follow," quoth young
      Lochinvar.

There was mounting 'mong Graemes of the Netherby clan;
Forsters, Fenwicks, and Musgraves, they rode and they ran:
There was racing and chasing on Canobie Lee,
But the lost bride of Netherby ne'er did they see.
So daring in love, and so dauntless in war,
Have ye e'er heard of gallant like young Lochinvar?

LOLLOCKS

Robert Graves

By sloth on sorrow fathered,
These dusty-feathered Lollocks
Have their nativity in all disordered
Backs of cupboard drawers.

They play hide and seek
Among collars and novels
And empty medicine bottles,
And letters from abroad
That never will be answered.

Every sultry night
They plague little children,
Gurgling from the cistern,
Humming from the air,
Skewing up the bed-clothes,
Twitching the blind.

When the imbecile agèd
Are over-long in dying
And the nurse drowses,
Lollocks come skipping
Up the tattered stairs
And are nasty together
In the bed's shadow.

The signs of their presence
Are boils on the neck,
Dreams of vexation suddenly recalled
In the middle of the morning,
Languor after food.

Men cannot see them,
Men cannot hear them,
Do not believe in them—
But suffer the more,
Both in neck and belly.

Women can see them—
O those naughty wives
Who sit by the fireside
Munching bread and honey,

Watching them in mischief
From corners of their eyes,
Slily allowing them to lick
Honey-sticky fingers.

Sovereign against Lollocks
Are hard broom and soft broom,
To well comb the hair,
To well brush the shoe,
And to pay every debt
So soon as it's due.

THE CAMEL'S HUMP (From *Just-So Stories*)
Rudyard Kipling

The Camel's hump is an ugly lump
    Which well you may see at the Zoo;
But uglier yet is the hump we get
    From having too little to do.

Kiddies and grown-ups too-oo-oo,
If we haven't enough to do-oo-oo,
      We get the hump—
      Cameelious hump—
The hump that is black and blue!

We climb out of bed with a frouzly head
    And a snarly-yarly voice.
We shiver and scowl and we grunt and we growl
    At our bath and our boots and our toys;

And there ought to be a corner for me
(And I know there is one for you)
      When we get the hump—
      Cameelious hump—
The hump that is black and blue!

The cure for this ill is not to sit still,
    Or frowst with a book by the fire;
But to take a large hoe and a shovel also,
    And dig till you gently perspire;

And then you will find that the sun and the wind,
And the Djinn of the Garden too,
      Have lifted the hump—
      The horrible hump—
The hump that is black and blue!

I get it as well as you-oo-oo—
If I haven't enough to do-oo-oo—
      We all get hump—
      Cameelious hump—
Kiddies and grown-ups too!

WHOLE DUTY OF CHILDREN

Robert Louis Stevenson

A child should always say what's true
And speak when he is spoken to,
And behave mannerly at table;
At least as far as he is able.

138

ON A TIRED HOUSEWIFE

Author Unknown

Here lies a poor woman who was always tired,
She lived in a house where help wasn't hired:
Her last words on earth were: 'Dear friends, I am going
To where there's no cooking, or washing, or sewing,
For everything there is exact to my wishes,
For where they don't eat there's no washing of dishes.
I'll be where loud anthems will always be ringing,
But having no voice I'll be quit of the singing.
Don't mourn for me now, don't mourn for me never,
I am going to do nothing for ever and ever.'

ADDRESS TO MY INFANT DAUGHTER
William Wordsworth

——Hast thou then survived——
Mild offspring of infirm humanity,
Meek infant! among all forlornest things
The most forlorn—one life of that bright star,
The second glory of the Heavens?—Thou hast.

EULALIE
Edgar Allan Poe

I dwelt alone
In a world of moan,
And my soul was a stagnant tide,
Till the fair and gentle Eulalie became my blushing bride—
Till the yellow-haired young Eulalie became my smiling
bride.

Ah less—less bright
The stars of the night
Than the eyes of the radiant girl!
And never a flake
That the vapour can make
With the moon-tints of purple and pearl,
Can vie with the modest Eulalie's most unregarded curl—
Can compare with the bright-eyed Eulalie's most humble
and careless curl.

140

Now Doubt—now Pain
Come never again,
For her soul gives me sigh for sigh,
And all the day long
Shines bright and strong
Astarte within the sky,
While ever to her dear Eulalie upturns her matron eye—
While ever to her young Eulalie upturns her violet eye.

THE LAND OF COUNTERPANE

Robert Louis Stevenson

When I was sick and lay a-bed,
I had two pillows at my head,
And all my toys beside me lay
To keep me happy all the day.

And sometimes for an hour or so
I watched my leaden soldiers go,
With different uniforms and drills,
Among the bed-clothes, through the hills;

And sometimes sent my ships in fleets
All up and down among the sheets;
Or brought my trees and houses out,
And planted cities all about.

I was the giant great and still
That sits upon the pillow-hill,
And sees before him, dale and plain,
The pleasant land of counterpane.

ARCHY CONFESSES

Don Marquis

coarse
jocosity
catches the crowd
shakespeare
and i
are often
low browed

the fish wife
curse
and the laugh
of the horse
shakespeare
and i
are frequently
coarse

aesthetic
excuses
in bills behalf
are adduced
to refine
big bills
coarse laugh

but bill
he would chuckle
to hear such guff
he pulled

rough stuff
and he liked
rough stuff

hoping you
are the same
        archy

From *VAUDRACOUR AND JULIA*
William Wordsworth

       To a lodge that stood
Deep in a forest, with leave given, at the age
Of four-and-twenty summers he withdrew;
And thither took with him his motherless Babe,
And one domestic for their common needs,
An aged woman. It consoled him here
To attend upon the orphan, and perform
Obsequious services to the precious child,
Which, after a short time, by some mistake
Or indiscretion of the Father, died.

From *A SHROPSHIRE LAD*
A. E. Housman

Into my heart an air that kills
    From yon far country blows:
What are those blue remembered hills,
    What spires, what farms are those?

That is the land of lost content,
      I see it shining plain,
The happy highways where I went
      And cannot come again.

THE JUMBLIES

Edward Lear

They went to sea in a sieve, they did;
      In a sieve they went to sea:
In spite of all their friends could say,
On a winter's morn, on a stormy day,
      In a sieve they went to sea.
And when the sieve turned round and round,
And every one cried, "You'll all be drowned!"
They called aloud, "Our sieve ain't big;
But we don't care a button; we don't care a fig:
      In a sieve we'll go to sea!"
            Far and few, far and few,
                  Are the lands where the Jumblies live:
                  Their heads are green, and their hands are blue;
                  And they went to sea in a sieve.

They sailed away in a sieve, they did,
      In a sieve they sailed so fast,
With only a beautiful pea-green veil
Tied with a ribbon, by way of a sail,
      To a small tobacco-pipe mast.
And every one said who saw them go,
"Oh! won't they be soon upset, you know?

For the sky is dark, and the voyage is long;
And, happen what may, it's extremely wrong
    In a sieve to sail so fast."

The water it soon came in, it did;
    The water it soon came in:
So, to keep them dry, they wrapped their feet
In a pinky paper all folded neat:
    And they fastened it down with a pin.
And they passed the night in a crockery jar;
And each of them said, "How wise we are!
Though the sky be dark, and the voyage be long
Yet we never can think we were rash or wrong,
    While round in our sieve we spin."

And all night long they sailed away;
    And, when the sun went down,
They whistled and warbled a moony song
To the echoing sound of a coppery gong,
    In the shade of the mountains brown,
"O Timballoo! How happy we are
When we live in a sieve and a crockery jar!
And all night long, in the moonlight pale,
We sail away with a pea-green sail
    In the shade of the mountains brown."

They sailed to the Western Sea; they did,—
    To a land all covered with trees:
And they bought an owl, and a useful cart,
And a pound of rice, and a cranberry-tart,
    And a hive of silvery bees;
And they bought a pig, and some green jackdaws,

And a lovely monkey with lollipop paws,
And forty bottles of ring-bo-ree,
    And no end of Stilton cheese:

And in twenty years they all came back,—
    In twenty years or more;
And every one said, "How tall they've grown.
For they've been to the Lakes, and the Torrible Zone,
    And the hills of the Chankly Bore."
And they drank their health, and gave them a feast
Of dumplings made of beautiful yeast;
And every one said, "If we only live,
We, too, will go to sea in a sieve,
    To the hills of the Chankly Bore."
        Far and few, far and few,
           Are the lands where the Jumblies live:
           Their heads are green, and their hands are blue;
           And they went to sea in a sieve.

I NEVER SAW A MOOR

Emily Dickinson

I never saw a moor,
I never saw the sea;
Yet know I how the heather looks,
And what a wave must be.

I never spoke with God,
Nor visited in Heaven;
Yet certain am I of the spot
As if the chart were given.

146

A SUBALTERN'S LOVE-SONG

John Betjeman

Miss J. Hunter Dunn, Miss J. Hunter Dunn,
Furnish'd and burnish'd by Aldershot sun,
What strenuous singles we played after tea,
We in the tournament—you against me!

Love-thirty, love-forty, oh! weakness of joy,
The speed of a swallow, the grace of a boy,
With carefullest carelessness, gaily you won,
I am weak from your loveliness, Joan Hunter Dunn.

147

Miss Joan Hunter Dunn, Miss Joan Hunter Dunn,
How mad I am, sad I am, glad that you won.
The warm-handled racket is back in its press,
But my shock-headed victor, she loves me no less.

Her father's euonymus shines as we walk,
And swing past the summer-house, buried in talk,
And cool the verandah that welcomes us in
To the six-o'clock news and a lime-juice and gin.

The scent of the conifers, sound of the bath,
The view from my bedroom of moss-dappled path,
As I struggle with double-end evening tie,
For we dance at the Golf Club, my victor and I.

On the floor of her bedroom lie blazer and shorts
And the cream-coloured walls are be-trophied with sports,
And westering, questioning settles the sun
On your low-headed window, Miss Joan Hunter Dunn.

The Hillman is waiting, the light's in the hall,
The pictures of Egypt are bright on the wall,
My sweet, I am standing beside the oak stair
And there on the landing's the light on your hair.

By roads "not adopted", by woodlanded ways,
She drove to the club in the late summer haze,
Into nine-o'clock Camberley, heavy with bells
And mushroomy, pine-woody, evergreen smells.

Miss Joan Hunter Dunn, Miss Joan Hunter Dunn,
I can hear from the car-park the dance has begun.
Oh! full Surrey twilight! importunate band!
Oh! strongly adorable tennis-girl's hand!

148

Around us are Rovers and Austins afar,
Above us, the intimate roof of the car,
And here on my right is the girl of my choice,
With the tilt of her nose and the chime of her voice,

And the scent of her wrap, and the words never said,
And the ominous, ominous dancing ahead.
We sat in the car park till twenty to one
And now I'm engaged to Miss Joan Hunter Dunn.

THE LITTLE CREATURE

Walter de la Mare

Twinkum, twankum, twirlum, twitch—
My great grandam—She was a Witch,
Mouse in Wainscot, Saint in niche—
My great grandam—She was a Witch;
Deadly nightshade flowers in a ditch—
My great grandam—She was a Witch;
Long though the shroud, it grows stitch by stitch—
My great grandam—She was a Witch;
Wean your weakling before you breech—
My great grandam—She was a Witch;
The fattest pig's but a double flitch—
My great grandam—She was a Witch;
Nightjars rattle, owls scritch—
My great grandam—She was a witch.

Pretty and small,
A mere nothing at all,
Pinned up sharp in the ghost of a shawl,
She'd straddle her down to the kirkyard wall,
And mutter and whisper and call,
And call . . .

Red blood out and black blood in,
My Nannie says I'm a child of sin.
How did I choose me my witchcraft kin?
Know I as soon as dark's dreams begin
Snared is my heart in a nightmare's gin;
Never from terror I out may win;
So—dawn and dusk—I pine, peak, thin,
Scarcely beknowing t'other from which—
My great grandam—She was a Witch.

"JIM, WHO RAN AWAY FROM HIS NURSE, AND WAS EATEN BY A LION"

Hilaire Belloc

There was a Boy whose name was Jim;
His Friends were very good to him.
They gave him Tea, and Cakes, and Jam,
And slices of delicious Ham,
And Chocolate with pink inside,
And little Tricycles to ride,
And read him Stories through and through,
And even took him to the Zoo—
But there it was the dreadful Fate
Befell him, which I now relate.

150

You know—at least you *ought* to know,
For I have often told you so—
That Children never are allowed
To leave their Nurses in a Crowd;
Now this was Jim's especial Foible,
He ran away when he was able,
And on this inauspicious day
He slipped his hand and ran away!
He hadn't gone a yard when—

                        Bang!

With open Jaws, a Lion sprang,
And hungrily began to eat
The Boy: beginning at his feet.

Now just imagine how it feels
When first your toes and then your heels,
And then by gradual degrees,
Your shins and ankles, calves and knees,
Are slowly eaten, bit by bit.
No wonder Jim detested it!
No wonder that he shouted "Hi!"
The Honest Keeper heard his cry,
Though very fat he almost ran
To help the little gentleman.
"Ponto!" he ordered as he came
(For Ponto was the Lion's name),
"Ponto!" he cried, with angry Frown.
"Let go, Sir! Down, Sir! Put it down!"
The Lion made a sudden Stop,
He let the Dainty Morsel drop,
And slunk reluctant to his Cage,
Snarling with Disappointed Rage.
But when he bent him over Jim,

The Honest Keeper's
                    Eyes were dim.
The Lion having reached his Head,
The Miserable Boy was dead!

When Nurse informed his Parents, they
Were more Concerned than I can say:—
His Mother, as She dried her eyes,
Said, "Well—it gives me no surprise,
He would not do as he was told!"
His Father, who was self-controlled,
Bade all the children round attend
To James' miserable end,
And always keep a-hold of Nurse
For fear of finding something worse.

ALAS, ALACK

Walter de la Mare

Ann, Ann!
Come! quick as you can!
There's a fish that *talks*
        In the frying pan.
Out of the fat,
        As clear as glass,
He put up his mouth
        And moaned 'Alas!'
Oh, most mournful,
        'Alas, alack!'
Then turned to his sizzling,
        And sank him back.
152

THE LITTLE TIPPLER

Emily Dickinson

I taste a liquor never brewed,
From tankards scooped in pearl;
Not all the vats upon the Rhine
Yield such an alcohol!

Inebriate of air am I,
And debauchee of dew,
Reeling, through endless summer days,
From inns of molten blue.

When landlords turn the drunken bee
Out of the foxglove's door,
When butterflies renounce their drams,
I shall but drink the more!

Till seraphs swing their snowy hats,
And saints to windows run,
To see the little tippler
Leaning against the sun!

THE STORY OF LITTLE SUCK-A-THUMB

From the German of Heinrich Hoffman

One day, mamma said: "Conrad dear,
I must go out and leave you here.
But mind now, Conrad, what I say,
Don't suck your thumb while I'm away.
The great tall tailor always comes
To little boys that suck their thumbs;
And ere they dream what he's about,
He takes his great sharp scissors out
And cuts their thumbs clean off,—and then,
You know, they never grow again."

Mamma had scarcely turned her back,
The thumb was in, alack! alack!
The door flew open, in he ran,
The great, long, red-legged scissors-man.
Oh, children, see! the tailor's come
And caught our little Suck-a-Thumb.
Snip! snap! snip! the scissors go;
And Conrad cries out—"Oh! oh! oh!"

Snip! snap! snip! They go so fast,
That both his thumbs are off at last.
Mamma comes home; there Conrad stands,
And looks quite sad, and shows his hands;—
"Ah!" said mamma, "I knew he'd come
To naughty little Suck-a-Thumb."

SEUMAS BEG

James Stephens

A man was sitting underneath a tree
Outside the village, and he asked me what
Name was upon this place, and said that he
Was never here before. He told a lot
Of stories to me too. His nose was flat.
I asked him how it happened, and he said
The first mate of the *Mary Ann* done that
With a marlin-spike one day, but he was dead,
And jolly good job too; and he'd have gone
A long way to have killed him, and he had
A gold ring in one ear; the other one
"Was bit off by a crocodile, bedad."
That's what he said. He taught me how to chew.
He was a real nice man. He liked me, too.

MY STAR

Robert Browning

All that I know
        Of a certain star
Is, it can throw
        (Like the angled spar)
Now a dart of red,
        Now a dart of blue,
Till my friends have said
        They would fain see, too,
My star that dartles the red and the blue!
Then it stops like a bird; like a flower, hangs furled:
    They must solace themselves with the Saturn above it.
What matter to me if their star is a world?
    Mine has opened its soul to me; therefore I love it.

CAPTAIN REECE

W. S. Gilbert

Of all the ships upon the blue
No ship contained a better crew
Than that of worthy CAPTAIN REECE,
Commanding of *The Mantelpiece.*

He was adored by all his men,
For worthy CAPTAIN REECE, R.N.,
Did all that lay within him to
Promote the comfort of his crew.

156

If ever they were dull or sad,
Their captain danced to them like mad,
Or told, to make the time pass by,
Droll legends of his infancy.

A feather bed had every man,
Warm slippers and hot-water can,
Brown windsor from the captain's store,
A valet, too, to every four.

Did they with thirst in summer burn?
Lo, seltzogenes at every turn,
And on all very sultry days
Cream ices handed round on trays.

Then currant wine and ginger pops
Stood handily on all the "tops";
And, also, with amusement rife,
A "Zoetrope, or Wheel of Life."

New volumes came across the sea
From MISTER MUDIE's libraree;
The Times and *Saturday Review*
Beguiled the leisure of the crew.

Kind-hearted CAPTAIN REECE, R.N.,
Was quite devoted to his men;
In point of fact, good CAPTAIN REECE
Beatified *The Mantelpiece.*

One summer eve, at half past ten,
He said (addressing all his men):

"Come, tell me, please, what I can do
To please and gratify my crew?

"By any reasonable plan
I'll make you happy, if I can;
My own convenience count as *nil*;
It is my duty, and I will."

Then up and answered WILLIAM LEE
(The kindly captain's coxswain he,
A nervous, shy, low-spoken man),
He cleared his throat and thus began:

"You have a daughter, CAPTAIN REECE,
Ten female cousins and a niece,
A ma, if what I'm told is true,
Six sisters, and an aunt or two.

"Now, somehow, sir, it seems to me,
More friendly-like we all should be
If you united of 'em to
Unmarried members of the crew.

"If you'd ameliorate our life,
Let each select from them a wife;
And as for nervous me, old pal,
Give me your own enchanting gal!"

Good CAPTAIN REECE, that worthy man,
Debated on his coxswain's plan:
"I quite agree," he said, "O BILL;
It is my duty, and I will.

"My daughter, that enchanting gurl,
Has just been promised to an earl,
And all my other familee,
To peers of various degree.

"But what are dukes and viscounts to
The happiness of all my crew?
The word I gave you I'll fulfil;
It is my duty and I will.

"As you desire it shall befall,
I'll settle thousands on you all,
And I shall be, despite my hoard,
The only bachelor on board."

The boatswain of *The Mantelpiece*,
He blushed and spoke to CAPTAIN REECE.
"I beg your honour's leave," he said,
"If you would wish to go and wed,

"I have a widowed mother who
Would be the very thing for you—
She long has loved you from afar,
She washes for you, Captain R."

The captain saw the dame that day—
Addressed her in his playful way—
"And did it want a wedding ring?
It was a tempting ickle sing!

"Well, well, the chaplain I will seek,
We'll all be married this day week—

At yonder church upon the hill;
It is my duty and I will!"

The sisters, cousins, aunts and niece,
And widowed ma of CAPTAIN REECE,
Attended there as they were bid;
It was their duty, and they did.

TREBETHERICK

John Betjeman

We used to picnic where the thrift
    Grew deep and tufted to the edge;
We saw the yellow foam-flakes drift
    In trembling sponges on the ledge
Below us, till the wind would lift
    Them up the cliff and o'er the hedge.
Sand in the sandwiches, wasps in the tea,
Sun on our bathing-dresses heavy with the wet,
Squelch of the bladder-wrack waiting for the sea,
Fleas round the tamarisk, an early cigarette.

From where the coastguard houses stood
    One used to see, below the hill,
The lichened branches of a wood
    In summer silver-cool and still;
And there the Shade of Evil could
    Stretch out at us from Shilla Mill.
Thick with sloe and blackberry, uneven in the light,
Lonely ran the hedge, the heavy meadow was remote,
The oldest part of Cornwall was the wood as black as night,
And the pheasant and the rabbit lay torn open at the throat.
160

But when a storm was at its height,
    And feathery slate was black in rain,
And tamarisks were hunt with light
    And golden sand was brown again,
Spring tide and blizzard would unite
    And sea came flooding up the lane.
Waves full of treasure then were roaring up the beach,
Ropes round our mackintoshes, waders warm and dry,
We waited for the wreckage to come swirling into reach,
Ralph, Vasey, Alastair, Biddy, John and I.

Then roller into roller curled
    And thundered down the rocky bay,
And we were in a water-world
    Of rain and blizzard, sea and spray,
And one against the other hurled
    We struggled round to Greenaway.
Blessed be St. Enodoc, blessed be the wave,
Blessed be the springy turf, we pray, pray to thee,
Give to our children all the happy days you gave
To Ralph, Vasey, Alastair, Biddy, John and me.

FOR EVERY EVIL . . .

Author Unknown

For every evil under the sun
There is a remedy, or there is none.
If there be one, try and find it;
If there be none, never mind it.

GOOD MASTER AND MISTRESS . . .

Author Unknown

Good master and mistress,
    While you're sitting by the fire,
Pray think of us poor children
    That wander in the mire.

We have got a little purse
    Made of leather skin,
We want a little money
    To line it well within.

Bring us out a table,
    And spread it with a cloth,
Bring us out a piece of cheese,
    And a pot of broth.

God bless the master of this house,
    Likewise the mistress too;
And all the little children
    That around the table go.

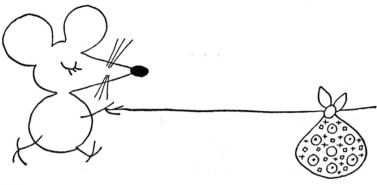

Good master and mistress,
    While you're sitting by the fire,
Pray think of us poor children
    Who are wandering in the mire.

A BALLAD OF JOHN SILVER

John Masefield

We were schooner-rigged and rakish, with a long and
        lissome hull,
And we flew the pretty colours of the cross-bones and the
        skull;
We'd a big black Jolly Roger flapping grimly at the fore,
And we sailed the Spanish Water in the happy days of yore.

We'd a long brass gun amidships, like a well-conducted
        ship,
We had each a brace of pistols and a cutlass at the hip;
It's a point which tells against us, and a fact to be deplored,
But we chased the goodly merchant-men and laid their ships
        aboard.

Then the dead men fouled the scuppers and the wounded
        filled the chains,
And the paint-work all was spatter-dashed with other
        people's brains,
She was boarded, she was looted, she was scuttled till she
        sank,
And the pale survivors left us by the medium of the plank.

163

O! then it was (while standing by the taffrail on the poop)
We could hear the drowning folk lament the absent chicken-
       coop;
Then, having washed the blood away, we'd little else to do
Than to dance a quiet hornpipe as the old salts taught us to.

O! the fiddle on the fo'c's'le, and the slapping naked soles,
And the genial 'Down the middle, Jake, and curtsey when
       she rolls!'
With the silver seas around us and the pale moon over
       head,
And the look-out not a-looking and his pipe-bowl glowing
       red.

Ah! the pig-tailed, quidding pirates and the pretty pranks
       we played,
All have since been put a stop-to by the naughty Board of
       Trade;
The schooners and the merry crews are laid away to rest,
A little south the sunset in the Islands of the Blest.

THE PLAINT OF THE CAMEL

Charles Edward Carryl

"Canary-birds feed on sugar and seed,
       Parrots have crackers to crunch;
And as for the poodles, they tell me the noodles
       Have chickens and cream for their lunch.
              But there's never a question
              About MY digestion—
       ANYTHING does for me!

164

"Cats, you're aware, can repose in a chair,
    Chickens can roost upon rails;
Puppies are able to sleep in a stable,
    And oysters can slumber in pails.
        But no one supposes
        A poor Camel dozes—
    ANYPLACE does for me!

"Lambs are enclosed where it's never exposed,
    Coops are constructed for hens;
Kittens are treated to houses well heated,
    And pigs are protected by pens.
        But a Camel comes handy
        Wherever it's sandy—
    ANYWHERE does for me!

"People would laugh if you rode a giraffe,
    Or mounted the back of an ox;
It's nobody's habit to ride on a rabbit,
    Or try to bestraddle a fox.
        But as for a Camel, he's
        Ridden by families—
    ANY LOAD does for me!

"A snake is as round as a hole in the ground,
    And weasels are wavy and sleek;
And no alligator could ever be straighter
    Than lizards that live in a creek,
        But a Camel's all lumpy
        And bumpy and humpy—
    ANY SHAPE does for me!"

THE PYTHON

Hilaire Belloc

A Python I should not advise,—
It needs a doctor for its eyes,
And has the measles yearly.
However, if you feel inclined
To get one (to improve your mind,
And not from fashion merely),
Allow no music near its cage;
And when it flies into a rage
Chastise it, most severely.
I had an aunt in Yucatan
Who bought a Python from a man
    And kept it for a pet.
She died, because she never knew
These simple little rules and few;—
    The Snake is living yet.

THE BANDOG

Walter de la Mare

Has anybody seen my Mopser?—
A comely dog is he,
With hair of the colour of a Charles the Fifth,
    And teeth like ships at sea,
His tail it curls straight upwards,
    His ears stand two abreast,
And he answers to the simple name of Mopser,
    When civilly addressed.

166

THE BELLS OF LONDON

Author Unknown

Gay go up and gay go down
To ring the bells of London town.

Bull's-eyes and targets,
Say the bells of St. Marg'rets.

Brick-bats and tiles,
Chime the bells of St. Giles!

Halfpence and farthings,
Ring the bells of St. Martin's.

Oranges and lemons,
Toll the bells of St. Clement's.

Pancakes and fritters,
Say the bells of St. Peter's.

Two sticks and an apple,
Say the bells of Whitechapel.

Old Father Baldpate,
Toll the slow bells of Aldgate.

Pokers and tongs,
Say the bells of St. John's.

Kettles and pans,
Say the bells at St. Ann's.

You owe me ten shillings,
Say the bells of St. Helen's.

When will you pay me?
Say the bells of Old Bailey.

When I grow rich,
Chime the bells of Shoreditch.

Pray when will that be?
Ask the bells of Stepney.

I'm sure I don't know,
Tolls the great bell at Bow.

Gay go up and gay go down
To ring the bells of London town.

THERE WAS A LITTLE GIRL . . .

Author Unknown

There was a little girl, who had a little curl
    Right in the middle of her forehead,
And when she was good, she was very, very good,
    But when she was bad she was horrid.

She stood on her head, on her little trundle-bed,
    With nobody by for to hinder;
She screamed and she squalled, she yelled and she bawled,
    And drummed her little heels against the winder.

168

Her mother heard the noise, and thought it was the boys
    Playing in the empty attic,
She rushed upstairs, and caught her unawares,
    And spanked her, most emphatic.

LIMERICK

Author Unknown

There was once a Young Lady of Ryde
Who ate a green apple and died;
    The apple fermented
    Inside the lamented,
And made cider inside her inside.

THE MOON'S THE NORTH WIND'S COOKY
(WHAT THE LITTLE GIRL SAID)

Vachel Lindsay

The Moon's the North Wind's cooky.
He bites it, day by day,
Until there's but a rim of scraps
That crumble all away.

The South Wind is a baker.
He kneads clouds in his den,
And bakes a crisp new moon *that . . . greedy*
North . . . Wind . . . eats . . . again!

I HAD A LITTLE HUSBAND . . .

Author Unknown

I had a little husband
  No bigger than my thumb;
I put him in a pint pot,
  And there I bade him drum.

I bought him a little horse,
  That galloped up and down;
I bridled him and saddled him,
  And sent him out of town.

I gave him some garters,
  To garter up his hose,
And a little handkerchief,
  To wipe his pretty nose.

170

THE COURTSHIP OF THE YONGHY-BONGHY-BO

Edward Lear

On the Coast of Coromandel
    Where the early pumpkins blow,
        In the middle of the woods
    Lived the Yonghy-Bonghy-Bo.
Two old chairs, and half a candle—
One old jug without a handle—
        These were all his worldly goods:
        In the middle of the woods,
        These were all the worldly goods,
    Of the Yonghy-Bonghy-Bo,
    Of the Yonghy-Bonghy-Bo.

Once, among the Bong-trees walking
    Where the early pumpkins blow,
        To a little heap of stones
    Came the Yonghy-Bonghy-Bo.
There he heard a Lady talking,
To some milk-white Hens of Dorking—
        " 'Tis the Lady Jingly Jones!
        On that little heap of stones
        Sits the Lady Jingly Jones!"
    Said the Yonghy-Bonghy-Bo,
    Said the Yonghy-Bonghy-Bo.

"Lady Jingly! Lady Jingly!
    Sitting where the pumpkins blow,
        Will you come and be my wife?"
    Said the Yonghy-Bonghy-Bo.

"I am tired of living singly—
On this coast so wild and shingly—
        I'm a-weary of my life;
        If you'll come and be my wife,
        Quite serene would be my life!"—
    Said the Yonghy-Bonghy-Bo,
    Said the Yonghy-Bonghy-Bo.

"On this Coast of Coromandel,
        Shrimps and watercresses grow,
            Prawns are plentiful and cheap,"
    Said the Yonghy-Bonghy-Bo.
"You shall have my chairs and candle,
And my jug without a handle!—
        Gaze upon the rolling deep
        (Fish is plentiful and cheap);
        As the sea, my love is deep!"
    Said the Yonghy-Bonghy-Bo,
    Said the Yonghy-Bonghy-Bo.

Lady Jingly answered sadly,
    And her tears began to flow—
        "Your proposal comes too late,
    Mr. Yonghy-Bonghy-Bo!
I would be your wife most gladly!"
(Here she twirled her fingers madly)
        "But in England I've a mate!
        Yes! you've asked me far too late,
        For in England I've a mate,
    Mr. Yonghy-Bonghy-Bo!
    Mr. Yonghy-Bonghy-Bo!

"Mr. Jones—(his name is Handel—
    Handel Jones, Esquire, & Co.)
        Dorking fowls delights to send,
    Mr. Yonghy-Bonghy-Bo!
Keep, oh! keep your chairs and candle,
And your jug without a handle—
        I can merely be your friend!
        —Should my Jones more Dorkings send,
        I will give you three, my friend!
    Mr. Yonghy-Bonghy-Bo!
    Mr. Yonghy-Bonghy-Bo!

"Though you've such a tiny body,
    And your head so large doth grow—
        Though your hat may blow away,
    Mr. Yonghy-Bonghy-Bo!
Though you're such a Hoddy Doddy—
Yet I wish that I could modi-
        fy the words I needs must say!

173

Will you please to go away?
That is all I have to say—
Mr. Yonghy-Bonghy-Bo!
Mr. Yonghy-Bonghy-Bo!

Down the slippery slopes of Myrtle,
    Where the early pumpkins blow,
        To the calm and silent sea
    Fled the Yonghy-Bonghy-Bo.
There, beyond the Bay of Gurtle,
Lay a large and lively Turtle—
        "You're the Cove," he said, "for me;
        On your back beyond the sea,
        Turtle, you shall carry me!"
    Said the Yonghy-Bonghy-Bo!
    Said the Yonghy-Bonghy-Bo!

Through the silent-roaring ocean
    Did the Turtle swiftly go;
        Holding fast upon his shell
    Rode the Yonghy-Bonghy-Bo.
With a sad primeval motion
Toward the sunset isles of Boshen
        Still the Turtle bore him well.
        Holding fast upon his shell,
        "Lady Jingly Jones, farewell!"
    Sang the Yonghy-Bonghy-Bo,
    Sang the Yonghy-Bonghy-Bo.

From the Coast of Coromandel,
    Did that Lady never go;
        On the heap of stones she mourns
    For the Yonghy-Bonghy-Bo.

On the Coast of Coromandel,
In his jug without a handle,
      Still she weeps, and daily moans,
      On that little heap of stones
      To her Dorking hens she moans,
    For the Yonghy-Bonghy-Bo,
    For the Yonghy-Bonghy-Bo.

UP AND DOWN THE CITY ROAD . . .
Author Unknown

Up and down the City Road,
    In and out the Eagle;
That's the way the money goes—
    Pop goes the weasel!

Half a pound of tuppenny rice,
    Half a pound of treacle;
Mix it up and make it nice—
    Pop goes the weasel!

Every night when I go out;
    The monkey's on the table;
Take a stick and knock it off—
    Pop goes the weasel!

INDEX OF AUTHORS

Aldis, Dorothy, 118
Allingham, William, 36

Belloc, Hilaire, 113, 150, 166
Bentley, E. C., 54
Betjeman, John, 147, 160
Bevington, Helen, 38
Bishop, Morris, 100
Blake, William, 32
Browning, Robert, 156
Bunyon, John, 96

Carroll, Lewis, 39, 52
Carryl, Charles Edward, 164
Chesterton, G. K., 16, 85
Chute, Marchette, 130
Ciardi, John, 40, 116
Coffin, Robert P. Tristram, 102
Coleridge, S. T., 101
Corbet, Richard, 61
Crane, Stephen, 41
cummings, e. e., 73

Davidson, John, 63
De la Mare, Walter, 86, 149, 152, 166
Dickinson, Emily, 146, 153
Drinkwater, John, 130

Eliot, T. S., 21, 35

Falstaff, Jake, 94
Fields, J. T., 82
Flecker, James Elroy, 114

Frost, Robert, 14, 89
Fyleman, Rose, 31

Gilbert, W. S., 125, 156
Gordon, George, Lord Byron, 50, 71
Graves, Robert, 17, 135
Guiterman, Arthur, 76

Hardy, Thomas, 42, 56
Hawker, R. S., 109
Herbert, A. P., 132
Herrick, Robert, 15
Hodgson, Ralph, 105
Hoffenstein, Samuel, 92
Hoffman, Heinrich, 154
Housman, A. E., 143
Hunt, Leigh, 124

Johnson, Samuel, 52

Kingsley, Charles, 48
Kipling, Rudyard, 120, 137

Lear, Edward, 103, 144, 171
Lindsay, Vachel, 170
Lytton, Robert, 47

Marquis, Don, 29, 104, 142
Masefield, John, 68, 163
McGonagall, William, 78, 99
Millay, Edna St. Vincent, 78
Moore, Julia, 122
Morley, Christopher, 54
Mother Goose, 70, 73

Nash, Ogden, 20, 112

Owen, Wilfred, 81

Peacock, Thomas Love, 110
Poe, Edgar Allan, 140
Preston, Keith, 124

Raleigh, Sir Walter, 93
Ransom, John Crowe, 21
Richards, Laura E., 72
Robinson, Edwin Arlington, 66

Sandburg, Carl, 117
Scott, Sir Walter, 13, 133
Scott, William Bell, 24

Shakespeare, William, 44
Skelton, John, 94
Stephens, James, 155
Stevenson, Robert Louis, 138, 141
Suckling, Sir John, 112
Swinburne, A. C., 58

Tennyson, Alfred Lord, 117
Thomas, Dylan, 45
Turner, Nancy Byrd, 77

Whitman, Walt, 44
Williams, William Carlos, 115
Wordsworth, William, 32, 51, 140,
 143

INDEX OF TITLES

Address to My Infant Daughter, 140

Alas, Alack, 152

And Shall Trelawny Die?, 109

Anthem for Doomed Youth, 81

anyone lived in a pretty how town, 73

archy confesses, 142

Ariel's Dirge, 44

Ashtabula Disaster, The, 122

Atalanta in Calydon, Chorus from, 58

Ballad of John Silver, A, 163

Bandog, The, 166

Barber, Barber, 57

Bells of London, The, 167

Bird's Nest, The, 130

Brown's Descent, 89

Camel's Hump, The, 137

Cape Ann, 35

Captain Reece, 156

Cervantes, 54

Colly, My Cow, 128

Conclusion, The, 93

Courtship of the Yonghy-Bonghy-Bo, The, 171

Cross Patch, 73

Curse on the Cat, A, 94

Darkling Thrush, The, 56

Death of Prince Leopold, The, 99

Destruction of Sennacherib, The, 50

Dick Johnson Reel, The, 94

1805, 17

Elegy in a Country Churchyard, 85

Eulalie, 140

Eve, 105

Fairies, The, 36

Farewell to the Fairies, 61

Farmer Went Trotting, A, 123

Fate if Unfair, 29

Fe, Fi, Fo, Fum, 116

Fern Hill, 45

For Every Evil, 161

Gardener's Song, The, 52

Going Back Again, 47

Good Master and Mistress, 162

Guests, 19

Hen and the Oriole, The, 104

Here Lies a Lady, 21

Hours of Idleness, 71

Humorist, The, 124

Hunter, The, 112

Hunting Song, 13

I Eat my Peas with Honey . . . , 72

I Had a Little Husband . . . , 170

I Never Saw a Moor, 146

I Took a Bow and Arrow, 116

Jenny Wren, 69

Jerusalem, 32

179

Jim, Who Ran Away from His Nurse . . . , 150
Jumblies, The, 144

Land of Counterpane, The, 141
Limerick, 169
Limericks, 103
Lion and the Unicorn, The, 85
Little Creature, The, 149
Little Green Orchard, The, 86
Little Tippler, The, 153
Llama, The, 113
Lochinvar, 133
Lollocks, 135
Looking-Glass, The, 120
Lyke-Wake Dirge, A, 107

Man from Porlock, The, 38
Man Saw a Ball of Gold in the Sky, A, 41
Merry Month of March, The, 32
Mice, 31
Mr. Flood's Party, 66
Moon's the North Wind's Cooky, The, 170
My Star, 156

Noiseless Patient Spider, A, 44
Nuts an' May, 119

Oh, the Funniest Thing . . . , 68
Old Buccaneer, The, 48
Old Men, 20
Old Mother Shuttle, 81
Old Quin Queeribus, 77
Old Ships, The, 114
Old Song Re-sung, An, 68
On a Tired Housewife, 139
One Bright Morning . . . , 132
Our Silly Little Sister, 118
Owl and the Eel and the Warming Pan, The, 72

Owl-Critic, The, 82

Pilgrim, The, 96
Plaint of the Camel, The, 164
Poems in Praise of Practically Nothing, Excerpt from, 92
Potomac Town in February, 117
Presents, 130
Prodigy, The, 132
Python, The, 166

Recuerdo, 78
Road Not Taken, The, 14
Rolling English Road, The, 16
Rum Tum Tugger, The, 21
Runnable Stag, A, 63

Seumas Beg, 155
Shakespearean Bear, The, 76
Shropshire Lad, A, Excerpt from, 143
Sneeze on a Monday . . . , 19
Spring and All, 115
Story of Little Suck-a-Thumb, The, 154
Story of Rimini, The, Excerpt from, 124
Subaltern's Love-song, A, 147
Swans Sing . . . , 101

Tay Bridge Disaster, The, 78
There Was a Little Girl . . . , 168
There Was an Old Woman . . . , 100
The Thorn, Excerpt from, 51
To Christopher North, 117
To Daffodils, 15
Tom o'Bedlam's Song, 97
Translations from the Chinese, Excerpts from, 54
Trebetherick, 160
Turnip Seller, The, 52

Up and down the City Road, 175

Vaudracour and Julia, Excerpt
from, 143
Voice of the Lobster, The, 39

War Song of Dinas Vawr, The, 110
Way down South . . . , 75
We Have Been Here Before, 100
Weathers, 42

What You Will Learn about the
Brobinyak, 40
When Jacky's a Very Good Boy, 70
Whole Duty of Children, The, 138
Why So Pale and Wan?, 112
Witch's Ballad, The, 24
Wraggle Taggle Gipsies, The, 33

Yankee Cradle, 102
Yarn of the *Nancy Bell,* The, 125

INDEX OF FIRST LINES

A child should always say what's true, 138
A farmer went trotting upon his grey mare, 123
A good sword and a trusty hand!, 109
A man was sitting underneath a tree, 155
A noiseless patient spider, 44
A Python I should not advise, 166
Alas! noble Prince Leopold, he is dead!, 99
All that I know, 156
And did those feet in ancient time, 32
And they had fixed the wedding day, 51
And while my visitor prattled, 55
Ann, Ann!, 152
anyone lived in a pretty how town, 73
At Viscount Nelson's lavish funeral, 17

Barber, barber, shave a pig, 57
Beautiful Railway Bridge of the Silv'ry Tay!, 78
Before the Roman came to Rye or out to Severn strode, 16
Brown lived at such a lofty farm, 89
By sloth on sorrow fathered, 135

"Canary-birds feed on sugar and seed, 164
coarse (jocosity catches the crowd), 142
Cross patch, 73

Eve, with her basket, was, 105
Even such is Time, that takes in trust, 93

Fair daffodils, we weep to see, 15
Farewell rewards and fairies, 61
Fe, fi, fo, fum, 116
For every evil under the sun, 161
From the hag and hungry goblin, 97
Full fathom five thy father lies;, 44

183

Gay go up and gay go down, 167
Good master and mistress, 162

Has anybody seen my Mopser?—, 166
—Hast thou then survived—, 140
Have you heard of the dreadful fate, 122
He must not laugh at his own wheeze:, 124
He thought he saw an Elephant, 52
Here lies a lady of beauty and high degree., 21
Here lies a poor woman who was always tired, 139
Here we come gathering nuts an' may, 119

I dream'd that I walk'd in Italy, 47
I dwelt alone, 140
I eat my peas with honey;, 72
I had a little husband, 166
I have seen old ships sail like swans asleep, 114
I kissed my darling at the Zoo, 132
I know a place, in the ivy on a tree, 130
I leant upon a coppice gate, 56
I never saw a moor, 146
I taste a liquor never brewed, 153
I think mice, 31
I took a bow and arrow, 116
I wanted a rifle for Christmas, 170
If a man who turnips cries, 52
in many places here and, 29
Into my heart an air that kills, 143
It is queer to think that many people, 55

Jenny Wren fell sick;, 69

Little Tom Dogget, 128

Miss J. Hunter Dunn, Miss J. Hunter Dunn, 147

Now as I was young and easy under the apple boughs, 45

O cat of churlish kind, 94
O I hae come from far away, 24
O quick quick quick, quick hear the song-sparrow, 35

184

O, young Lochinvar is come out of the west, 133
Of all the ships upon the blue, 156
Oh England is a pleasant place for them that's rich and high, 48
Oh, the funniest thing I've ever seen, 68
Old Dick Johnson, gentleman, adventurer, 94
Old Eben Flood, climbing alone one night, 66
Old Mother Shuttle, 81
Old Quin Queeribus—, 77
On the Coast of Coromandel, 171
One bright morning in the middle of the night, 132
One day, mamma said: "Conrad dear, 154

People expect old men to die, 20

Queen Bess was Harry's daughter. Stand forward partners all!, 120

Ready she sat with one hand to turn o'er, 124

Sneeze on a Monday, you sneeze for danger;, 19
So lucky I was in being born, 102
so much depends, 115
Some one is always sitting there, 86
Swans sing before they die—'twere no bad thing, 101

The Assyrian came down like the wolf on the fold, 50
The bridge says: Come across, try me; see how good I am, 117
The Brobinyak has Dragon Eyes, 40
The Camel's hump is an ugly lump, 137
The cock is crowing, 32
The hunter crouches in his blind, 112
The Llama is a woolly sort of fleecy hairy goat, 113
The man knocked strongly at the door, 38
The men that worked for England, 85
The Moon's the North Wind's cooky, 170
The mountain sheep are sweeter, 110
The owl and the eel and the warming-pan, 72
The people of Spain think Cervantes, 54
The Rum Tum Tugger is a Curious Cat:, 21
There was a Boy whose name was Jim;, 150
There was a little girl, who had a little curl, 168

There was an Old Man of The Hague, 103
There was an old woman tossed up in a basket, 100
There was once a Young Lady of Ryde, 169
There were three gipsies a-come to my door, 33
They went to sea in a sieve, they did;, 144
This ae nighte, this ae nighte, 107
This is the weather the cuckoo likes, 42
'Tis the voice of the Lobster; I heard him declare, 39
To a lodge that stood, 143
To begin with she wouldn't have fallen in, 118
'Twas on the shores that round our coast, 125
Twinkum, twankum, twirlum, twitch—, 149
Two roads diverged in a yellow wood, 14

Up and down the City Road, 175
Up the airy mountain, 36

Waken, lords and ladies gay, 13
Way down South where bananas grow, 75
We used to picnic where the thrift, 160
We were schooner-rigged and rakish, with a long and lissome hull, 163
We were very tired, we were very merry—, 78
well boss did it, 104
What passing-bells for these who die as cattle?, 81
When Friendship or Love our sympathies move, 71
When I was sick and lay a-bed, 141
When Jacky's a very good boy, 70
When, on our casual way, 76
When I visited America, 54
When the hounds of spring are on winter's traces, 58
When the pods went pop on the broom, green broom, 63
'Who stuffed that white owl?' No one spoke in the shop., 82
Who would true valour see, 96
Why so pale and wan, fond lover?, 112

Yet if His Majesty, our sovereign lord, 19
You did late review my lays, 117
You take a bath, and sit there bathing, 92
Youth is conservative, 54

186